FRE

David R. Mueller
1974

BOOKS BY HENRIETTA BUCKMASTER

NOVELS
All the Living
And Walk in Love
Bread from Heaven
Fire in the Heart
Deep River
His End Was His Beginning
Tomorrow Is Another Day

HISTORY
*Let My People Go: A History of the
Anti-slavery Movement and the Underground Railroad*

CHILDREN'S BOOKS
The Seminole Wars
Walter Raleigh: Man of Two Worlds
Flight to Freedom
Lucy and Loki

FREEDOM

BOUND

✪

✪

by Henrietta Buckmaster

COLLIER BOOKS, NEW YORK

FOR
PAUL WOHL CUM NINA AND ZENOBIA

First Collier Books Edition 1967

Freedom Bound was originally published in
a hardcover edition by the Macmillan Company

The Macmillan Company, New York
Collier-Macmillan Canada Ltd., Toronto, Ontario

PRINTED IN THE UNITED STATES OF AMERICA

INTRODUCTION

THIS is not an objective book.

Whatever the value of objectivity—and we can certainly enumerate these values with appreciation—it is not a condition which should be raised to a way of life.

Life is for living. It is not for looking at, or being disposed toward; it is in no sense a grammatical locution. Life is an ethos. It is a reciprocal experience. It is the demand to be *whole*. All the methodologies of historians are so many hollow echoes in an empty place, returning precisely the sounds dispensed—unless they are concerned with living.

History is made for man, not man for history. For a few years a handful of states in the southern part of the United States endeavored to find a way of mutual purpose, struggled to create a common amity among the human beings living within their borders. They used the desperate inadequate tools at hand because they had no others, and those years are so replete with the inner and outer lives of men, women, and children, so filled with living voices, so intense with hope, despair, mistakes, fulfillments, that they simply nullify any foolish exercise of the objective.

But, then, there has never been an objective book about the Reconstruction period. It demands friends or enemies. Perhaps because it does not belong on the library shelves, perhaps because it is an integral part of our unfinished business—a clamorous present needs to understand that if an individual is cut off in any of his parts he does not function well as a man, and all other members of the human family suffer in proportion.

Reconstruction, in its conventional meaning, was narrowly exemplified in two southern states which had a Negro majority in state and legislature, in four which had a Negro balance of power. The longest tenure was in South Carolina—seven years. The shortest, in North Carolina—two. No period in Virginia, two military occupations in Georgia to enforce majority rule. In Florida, Louisiana, Alabama, and Mississippi, Reconstruction fought to survive for half a decade.

When it came to an end, many of the public and private records were destroyed by carelessness as well as by a desire to expunge evidence of the consequences of social revolution. But the legislation which had become state law was in most cases too good to be repealed immediately. It stayed on the statute books until it became such an anachronism in the segregated world of the 1880's and 1890's that it had to go.

═══════════

WITH Appomattox, four million black people in the South owned their skins and nothing more.

Eleven million white people in the South owned their wounds, their bewilderment, and their willingness to take a look at the future.

This left the old oligarchy of slaveholders, that quarter of a million white people who had ruled Congress for two generations, and they were determined that nothing should cancel their power in the past or trick them out of power in the future.

It was a small percentage to speak so loudly and claim to make history.

In early April 1865, when the air was redolent with spring and the smell of unburied men and horses, each officer and man of the broken Confederate army was put under parole and allowed to return to his home. Those who had horses were allowed to keep them. It was a generous provision for the vanquished. It was designed to set the tone for a peaceful future.

But four million black men and women had been at the heart of the conflict. They were the true pulse and beat of peace.

There had been some talk of shipping them all out of the country when the war ended. Logistics and some elemental good sense intervened. Only the last grip of insanity could pretend that Negro Americans were not among the oldest Americans.

With compassion and hope, with torn fields and burgeoning meadows, with young mules and old carts given new life with a string and a prayer, everyone started on his way to the future. Poor white and colored men without land were not looking behind but ahead.

Men like Horace Greeley, who edited the *New York Tribune* and made up most of his reforms out of his head, were convinced that the Negroes, throwing off slavery, would become citizens by a kind of "natural process—industry on their part balanced by white acceptance of them as political equals." A community of spontaneous equality would live happily ever after.

Other men had a tougher vision based on instincts of justice and economic reality, a small vision perhaps, because democracy itself had had a poor show in a country half-slave and half-free. These were the men who had brought the anti-slavery agitation from a small moral outcry to a North-wide protest based on free labor and modern industry.

Take Thaddeus Stevens, for example. He had been a representative from Pennsylvania since 1849. He had fought for the rights of man—any shape, size, or color of man—for thirty years. On principle he was tough and remorseless. He had political genius. He was also, as Carl Sandburg has said, "at his best, a majestic and isolated figure wandering in an ancient wilderness thick with thorns seeking to bring justice between man and man." "He had a will of inherent and uncommon might," a friend said of him, "a perfect indifference to praise or blame, an invincible and incorruptible moral sense"—and this moral sense never shifted on Negro rights and citizenship. He also had a wit that could take the skin off a man.

Stevens had not let the war obscure the reasons for the war. Men might cry, "Preserve the Union!" but he asked what but slavery had ever threatened the Union? This was empiricism with a sting.

He seemed quite unaffected by praise or blame; to be

without intellectual or personal vanity. (He wore an old black wig and when an admiring lady once asked for a lock of his hair, he took off the wig and offered it to her.) As majority leader he ruled the Republican members of the House with an iron hand. "Rarely wounded in any contest," a colleague wrote, "his wounds never bled but healed without scars as he had no memory of the blows he provoked or received, still less apology or regret for those he had given."

He had spent the war colliding with the slow motions of political contingencies. In July 1861 he had begun to pummel Congress with a series of bills designed to show that the North *did* intend to free the slaves. The bills got nowhere. In November he introduced a bill asking for total emancipation. It was defeated. In December he asked Lincoln to free every slave who bought his own freedom. (Union generals were sending fugitives who escaped to the Union lines back into slavery.) That week Lincoln suggested to Congress that the border states agree to abolish slavery by the year 1900. A man "with the slows," it was said of him!

But Lincoln did not believe that Congress had power to alter any condition within a state—even slavery. A constitutional amendment, ratified state by state, would be the only way to kill slavery.

By 1862 Stevens was close to despair. He and his anti-slavery colleagues thought the war would drift to an end, slavery as strong as ever, and peace a long twilight of hope. He saw Lincoln as honest and amiable but under the control of the border states men and of "negro-phobic counsels" within and without his Cabinet. Stevens could not see Lincoln's heart nor the "great impulse moving him to do justice to five or six million people."

By now, the Negroes' vigorous participation in their own freedom was affecting the whole conduct of the war. In the North, a hundred and forty-four Negro delegates met in a convention in Syracuse, New York. They spoke for the free Negroes of eighteen states, seven of them within the Confederacy. The delegates organized the National Equal Rights League and petitioned Congress to remove "invidious distinctions" based upon color, to recruit Negro troops with equal pay. They expressed their thanks to the President and to Congress for authorizing Negro mail carriers, for abolishing slavery in the District of Columbia, for recognizing the Negro republics of Liberia and Haiti.

Frederick Douglass, the great Negro, had the power to state a profound fact simply. He said to Lincoln: "The colored race can never be respected anywhere till respected in America."

By 1863, slaves were pouring into Union camps (the officers no longer allowed to turn them away). Twenty thousand refugees were in the District of Columbia, 50,000 in North Carolina, 50,000 in South Carolina, others in Georgia, in Louisiana. The Valley of the Mississippi had camps sheltering over 500,000. They worked for the army, for wages, building fortifications and roads. They wanted to fight. They begged for regiments. The agitation for Negro soldiers became a moral and practical necessity. After the Emancipation Proclamation in 1863, Stevens began congressional pressure for the enlistment of Negroes. Once more Lincoln waited to hear what the country would say.

Negro officers command white men? Stevens answered sardonically that his bill authorized only soldiers and noncommissioned officers, for "I do not expect to live to see the day when, in this Christian land, merit shall counterbalance the crime of color."

But Lincoln knew the necessity not only to bring desperately needed manpower to the Union army but to increase morale as well. Stevens' only real fight was for equal pay. This was the nakedest kind of justice . . . Negro soldiers knew if they were captured they would be sold as fugitive slaves, not treated as prisoners of war. White offi-

4

cers commanding them would not be given the status of prisoners, but put to death as insurrectionists. (When Confederate General Nathan Bedford Forrest seized Fort Pillow in Tennessee, every Negro soldier and white officer was shot or clubbed or burned to death; not a prisoner was taken.)

For eighteen months the Negroes served without pay until put on an equal footing with white soldiers.

There were 179,000 Negro soldiers in the Union Army. One hundred thousand came from the South—the first four Negro regiments in the Union army recruited in Louisiana. Sixteen men received Congressional Medals of Honor.

Men who were killed together took on an equality. But what about the living? They needed land; they needed assurance of a future. Confiscation of land for the poor men of the South, colored and white, who had been the Union's friends was reasonable, but as an issue it was even more explosive than emancipation.

From the beginning of the war, the Radical Republicans had been aware that this essential issue of land lay at the heart of emancipation. In July 1862 Stevens had laid down a hard line from which he never retreated. "I would seize every foot of land and every dollar of property as our armies go along and put it to the uses of the war and the payment of our debts . . . I would sell Confederate lands to the soldiers of independence; I would send those soldiers with arms in their hands to occupy the heritage of traitors and build up there a land of free men and of freedom which, fifty years hence, could swarm with its hundreds of millions without a slave upon its soil."

Wendell Phillips, the great Abolitionist, had access to the nation's conscience, and he tried to water and nurture it. "While those large estates remain in the hands of the defeated slave oligarchy, its power is not destroyed. But let me confiscate the land of the South and put it into the hands of the Negroes and white men who have fought for

5

it and you may go to sleep with your parchments. I have planted a Union as sure to grow as an acorn to become an oak. You do not build governments like a clapboard house; you plant them like an oak. Plant a hundred thousand Negro farmers and by their side a hundred thousand white soldiers and I will risk the South."

But Lincoln could not hear. He himself might not consider a man's property more sacred than his life, but he had a nation devoted to private property to lead through a war. When a Confiscation Bill passed Congress in 1862 (directed mainly at freeing that animate property, the slave), he said he would veto it unless it made clear that the rebel owner did not lose his title to the land.

As the war came up the eastern coast, swarming over the Sea Islands of Georgia, Lincoln agreed that some of the captured plantations could be sold to pay taxes.

Sherman would have used the plantations anyway, for he had an army of refugees clinging to his command as he marched across Georgia. He authorized them to take possession of the land of the Sea Islands, and to work the rice plantations that ran inland for thirty miles. Four hundred eighty-five thousand acres were divided among 40,000 Negroes. It was a small revolution (promissory titles only were given), but the Union officers assured the Negroes that the land was theirs forever.

General Sherman also did something about education. When Edwin Stanton, the Secretary of War, came down to Savannah in December 1864, Sherman introduced him to a committee of eight or ten Negro clergymen of Savannah who wished to discuss the opening of schools. Stanton was impressed by them. He said their questions were "so shrewd, so wise and so comprehensive that they would have attracted attention in any assembly."

The decision was made to open schools as soon as teachers could be found. Sherman was astonished at the number of Negro men and women who presented themselves. The Reverend James Lynch, a remarkable Negro,

6

born in Baltimore of a free father and a slave mother (whose freedom was bought for her by her husband), helped the colored people of the city to organize the teaching. He had a degree from Kimball University in Hanover, New Hampshire, and had been sent South by the Methodist mission. He was joined by the Reverend J. W. Alvord of Boston, Secretary of the American Tract Society, who was soon to become commissioner of education for the Freedmen's Bureau. The two men examined teachers and at last found ten who qualified.

The next problem was to find a schoolhouse. They selected the old Bryan Slave Mart with which the Negroes had had such an intimate association, and the bars which divided the slave pens were knocked down to make room for the children's seats. Mr. Lynch always had an appropriately ironic sense of occasion, as he showed a few years later when he became secretary of state in Mississippi.

By December 1865, five hundred pupils were studying in Savannah schools and the Negroes had gathered a fund of one thousand dollars to help pay the teachers' expenses.

The irresistible thrust of men and war snatched many problems out of a theoretic realm. As Grant moved down the Mississippi, hundred of thousands of slaves begged—demanded—their part in the Union. Some arrived empty-handed; others arrived with the tools, mules, horses of their owners. Grant was no stony-heart. He set up help immediately, asked for volunteers among his officers. Around Memphis, where troops had access to rail transportation, swarms of terrified slaves refused to be left behind when the army moved. It became a familiar and poignant sight to see men, women, and children clinging to every inch of space on passenger and freight trains, even crouching and swaying on the tops of the cars. The engineers were instructed to move the trains as carefully as possible so as not to jar loose the clinging fingers.

As the army approached Vicksburg, thirty thousand

refugees stormed the lines. "The scenes were appalling," General John Eaton wrote to an antislavery friend. General Eaton had been made superintendent in charge of freedmen for the Department of the Tennessee. He was a man of great heart, great imagination, and great administrative talent. "The refugees were crowded together, sickly, disheartened, dying on the streets; no physicians, no medicines, no hospitals . . . the whites suffered as much as the blacks, and all were temporarily fed by the government . . . The great multitude were unprepared to work beyond supplying their immediate necessities. Their minds were not adjusted to the new situation. Southern prejudice against paying blacks was so great that it required almost superhuman efforts on the part of my officers to secure payment and trustworthiness in service. Our aim was, by the simplest principles and expedience, to bring labor and its rewards into their natural relations to the people."

It was a task of such heroic proportions that it has probably never been evaluated properly. Every step had to be improvised. The recruiting of officers was one of the biggest snags. To serve the Negro! Heaven forbid! Southern officers could not have been more shocked. Yet General Eaton knew that the love which went with service was indispensable to this vast "experiment in the interests of humanity." He himself was a man of infinite patience and compassion. He loved the light that came with education, he was determined that it should glow as quickly and as steadily as possible for all those under his care. He knew also how closely the experiment would be watched and how far it could reach into the future.

Civilian volunteers were the blood of the Department of Freedmen. Missionary societies were the first in the field —Presbyterians, Methodists, Congregationalists. Quakers were fast on their heels, too. These volunteers brought money, clothes, and their own tireless devotion. Women whose peacetime lives were conventional and protected arrived with their little handtrunks crammed with bandages and books. They asked to work in the refugee camps as quickly as possible.

White refugees were also coming by the thousands, most of them trying to escape the draft into the Confederate army. Cairo, Illinois, was organized as a portal through which whites and Negroes were sent North as fast as homes, employment, and army recruiting could be arranged.

But the majority of the Negroes remained in the Valley of the Mississippi. The commissioners of the Freedmen's Department felt that their first obligation was to make the Negro a self-supporting unit of society. General Eaton filled them with his own conviction that self-respect was the quickest training for citizenship.

Negro men were provided with arms to guard the camps. Each man was made responsible for his own family. This one act was a violent surgical operation, cutting away one of the most cancerous growths of slavery. For under slavery no man *had* a family. He might live with a woman in love and faithfulness all the days of his life and breed a family of children, but the threat of separation hung over them all the time. Slavery violated every principle of family life. No slave could be legally married and "husbands" were sold from their "wives." Children did not belong to their parents and could be swept away without warning. One of the most poignant sights in refugee camps was the search for "husbands," "wives," or children.

Legalized marriage was immediately offered to those slaves who arrived in families, and was as swiftly accepted. One day an army chaplain married a hundred and nineteen couples in a little over an hour. All of them were men and women who had lived together as best they could for many years. More than anything else, the ceremony of legal marriage seemed to make freedom real to the former slave.

Education came next in measuring manhood. Education had also been illegal for the slave, and new laws were invariably added after each large slave uprising. Yet many slaves could read and write. Clandestine schools and occasional slave owners' wives had lighted the way. Frederick Douglass taught himself by studying torn newspapers on the road. Slaves often stood outside the open windows of schools until they had mastered a lesson.

Louisiana was taken early by the Union forces, and General Nathaniel Banks had established a free school system for the Negroes. He required a school tax from all landowners who employed Negroes in the field. When Arkansas was occupied by General Steele in 1863, the Negroes in Little Rock formed a Freedmen's School Society, and by their own efforts made the city schools free for an entire year. By March 1865, the Valley of the Mississippi had 51 schools, 105 teachers, and an enrollment of 7,400 students. In the Department of the South, which included North and South Carolina and Georgia, General Rufus Saxton was also developing free education as rapidly as possible.

These schools were not the result of any abstract conviction on the part of the generals. The schools had come to life because the Negroes demanded it. A slave in a camp picked up a book. He believed that by grasping it he could become a new man by a kind of osmosis. The passion for education drew unwilling volunteers. Union officers became brusque and diffident teachers. White boy-soldiers, scarcely able to read themselves, matched out a sentence with a Negro father. The lady volunteers, however, had brought slates and pencils with them.

A report came into General Eaton's office. "I saw a small detachment of infantry soldiers (Negro) who had previously been unable to secure any attention from a teacher, placed within reach of a mission family. The soldiers had not been there an hour when those not on sentry had procured spelling books and begged one of the ladies to aid them; they soon were busily at work on the alphabet."

General Eaton at one time asked a tuition fee from each parent in an effort to improve the schools. It violated his concept of an American public school, but it was enthusiastically supported by the parents.

The fee ranged from $1.25 to twenty-five cents a month according to the ability of the parents to pay. Sometimes ten cents was paid. But no child was refused an education for lack of a fee. Attendance increased.

The responsibility and value which came with money made wages the third essential in measuring the reality of freedom. Paying wages to the Negro proved to be one of the most revolutionary of all undertakings.

The army could absorb many thousands of laborers in various departments, and many thousands—62,300 to be exact—found their own employment as mechanics, barbers, draymen, and so on. But the majority wanted land one way or another. When federal soldiers, swarming over the countryside around Jackson, Mississippi, in 1863, told the Negroes on a large plantation that they were free, the slaves immediately measured off the land with a plowline, dividing it equally among themselves, and apportioned the cotton and farm implements.

Whenever Union soldiers took a plantation, the slaves responded by measuring out tracts and setting pegs. Any patch of land was good enough if it would grow corn and cotton.

The government made quick use of this desire. They offered wages or a share of the crops if refugees would settle on abandoned plantations and produce the indispensable fruit of the land—food, crops, and cotton. Sometimes abandoned plantations were leased to the refugees for token payments. (In Congress, antislavery legislators felt the land should be confiscated and given to them forever. The Negroes felt the same way, and believed that time would work for them.)

At first the plantations near the Union camps were selected for resettlement, since a degree of protection could be offered the Negroes. But as more crops were needed, the Negroes themselves began to work the isolated and exposed lands. Guns were supplied them, and army patrols did what they could, but the hazard from guerrillas did not let up night or day.

Now and then white planters, caught behind the Union lines, were willing to take their places in history by hiring the field hands who, the day before, had been their slaves.

The chaos and suffering were indescribable. Military needs came first, but the devotion and imagination that was brought to the freedmen produced one miracle after the other.

Fixed wages were established, from government or private employer, and the freedmen's agents were demons when it came to enforcing this rule. The government's object was not to offer the best wages, but to encourage the greatest bargaining on the open market—and then to protect that bargain. The goal of the agents was to teach the nature and responsibility of citizenship, but sometimes the mere act of survival was the greatest lesson that could be learned. The imagination reels when one is asked to consider the range of responsibility and the almost insoluble problems to be resolved by a handful of men. Whenever the agents could combine practicality with idealism they were quick to do so.

For example, a tax was ordered (for a time) on the wages of Negro men. This tax was to care for the sick and dependent. It was a calculated risk by the Department. But the Negro wage earner approved it as he had approved the school fee. He saw it as the government's recognition of him as a man. He saw it as a power protecting his right to make a bargain and as a legal means of compelling the white man to pay his wages. (No wages—no tax; and both defaulters had to appear before a freedmen's agent.) He also said candidly that he liked the status which came from bearing the burden of his own poor and aged.

"This tax," wrote Eaton, "together with the funds accruing from the profits of labor in the Department, met all the incidental expenses of our widespread operations" —paid for hispitals, clothing, utensils, and tools for the Negro.

Washington redtape eventually corrupted the situation to such an extent that some of the work was brought to a halt. And the mischief was compounded when a Washington directive transferred the freedmen's activities from the army to the Treasury Department.

The Treasury Department required a show of profit. A show of profit was impossible if humane conditions were to be maintained and the Negro protected.

Eaton himself went to lay the matter before Lincoln. Lincoln cut through the redtape. Authority was returned to the army.

Grant supported and fought for the work from start to finish. He wanted to see successful Negro enterprises and he saw them. He wanted what he called a "Negro Paradise." At Davis Bend, Mississippi, an autonomous government was set up, with sheriffs and judges appointed from the Negro settlers, and all details of self-government learned through experience.

Confiscation of land would have been one of the quickest and surest ways of consolidating northern victories, but virtually no one in the government was prepared for such a step. Land distribution would have assisted the poor white farmers as much as the freed slave.

Along the eastern coast of Georgia and South Carolina, the abandoned lands were farmed under various arrangements. In exchange for small parcels, Negroes agreed to raise cotton on larger plantations set aside for this purpose. Occasionally they were able to buy or rent parcels of land confiscated for taxes. But around the eastern seaboard and in sections in Mississippi, speculators and northern contractors were gaining control of large areas of land and attempting to undercut the wages of the freedmen even while the guns were still blasting the trees and fields.

With the sole exception of the improvised program of the Department of Freedmen, developed on the spot day by day, not a single plan had been made to meet the vast social change that would come with the end of the war. Lincoln had ventured the proposal that a state could be received back into the Union if ten percent of its voters were loyal Union men. He ventured also the thought that the "educated" Negro or the soldier should be given the vote. Louisiana was made the test. Not only had New Orleans fallen early to the Union forces, but both General Butler and General Banks had been keenly aware of the quality of Negroes in that brilliant, lawless, Creole city. Many were educated; many were rich.

But when two white congressmen from Louisiana presented themselves in Washington in 1864, Stevens set all his power against them. True, they were Union men, but they also represented only one-fifth of the voters and this was a violation of democratic representation. And Negro suffrage, though agreed on in principle, had not been implemented.

When tentative state governments were set up on the ten percent basis in Tennessee and Arkansas, the Radical Republicans refused them all support. Virginia had split in the first year of the war. Beyond the mountains, in the west, Unionists made a new state, West Virginia. F. H. Pierpont became the first governor and, as the armies of the Potomac extended their control, he moved briefly to Alexandria. In May 1864, a constitution was adopted by one-tenth of Virginia voters with no mention of Negro suffrage. Lincoln recognized the government. Across the river friends were needed.

The tall man in Washington had a set of working principles which he constantly amplified. They might, because he had the knack, be turned into a workable policy. This was not an age of planning. If goodwill fitted necessity what more could one ask?

On January 31, 1865, Congress at length passed an amendment which, when ratified, would become the Thirteenth and render slavery illegal.

Charles Sumner, in the Senate from Massachusetts, was Stevens' only equal, though as different from him as spring from fall. Sumner was a scholar, a dandy, the most elegant man in Congress, dressed customarily in maroon vest, fawn gaiters, blue-violet neck scarves, high silk hat, magnificent cape, his gold-headed cane used like a scepter. He was over six feet tall, handsome, somewhat pompous, but never afraid to mention the unmentionable. The horrors and obscenities of slavery which no other senator would deal with were among Sumner's most powerful weapons. His fight against slavery had dominated his whole Senate career. In 1856, he had been so violently beaten over the head by a representative from South Carolina, as he sat pinned to his desk in the Senate, that it took him four years to recover.

Longfellow called him "a colossus holding his burning heart in his hand to light up the sea of life." Orotund, perhaps, but recognizable.

In February 1865, Sumner had made a powerful speech reminding the Senate that democracy now had a chance to operate in this republic for the first time. He made a passionate plea that under no circumstances should a man be deprived in the future of his right to vote because of race or color.

All persistent nudges in the mind, but not foregone conclusions even yet. The Radical Republicans knew the fight with Lincoln was only beginning. They knew Congress was made up of coalitions held to a single purpose only by the emergencies of war. They were not underestimating the fight nor Lincoln's political genius nor, in the end, his great heart.

"With his usual shrewdness and caution he is picking out the mortar from the points [of slavery] until eventually the whole tower will fall," Stevens said wryly.

But they also knew that unless the rights of the Negro were established without delay the fight would be cruel and protracted. For months before the end of the war, the North had been living in the future. The future meant a new, dazzling world impatiently waiting to blaze into trade, markets, westward expansion. Northern speculators were already swarming into those parts of the South held by the Union armies, bidding for land, eyeing the situation. If the freed Negro fitted into this future, fine. If he did not, he would become merely another detail in a swarming empiricism of unlimited promise and calculated surprise.

If the defeated Rebs fitted in, that too was fine as long as they did not rock the boat. No living in the past! No interference with manifest destiny!

The Radical Republicans knew all these things. But men like Sumner and Stevens, Ben Wade, Carl Schurz, Henry Wilson, wanted to know what "manifest destiny" meant for the Negro. What destiny awaited the four million who had been freed?

Free men had meant, heretofore, in the lexicon of the world, *white men*. The handful of Negroes—488,070 in 1860—who had bought their own freedom or who had been born free had been exotic figures in the days before the war. Those in the South had been made as contemptible as possible; in the North they had been fitted into a peripheral society only by the grace of other men's consciences. Now all Negroes were free. Now the word had to be pruned of all ambiguous meaning.

There were no industries in the South to absorb these four million freedmen. The land, the plows, the crops belonged to the white man—and that meant the white *minority* who had caused all the trouble. Was there hope as small as a man's fist that this minority would voluntarily surrender their rights in the land or in the laborers who had from time immemorial tended it? Would there be enough goodwill to reshape a society on the basis of political rights for all? Since no one really answered these burning questions except by circumlocutions, it was safe to assume that there was not much reason to hope.

Then a shot was fired in Washington on April 15, 1865, and a great man died.

When the immediate shock was over, the Radical Republicans held their breath and took a long look at the new President. Andrew Johnson had made many statements more forthright than Lincoln's. In February 1864, he had spoken to a torchlight crowd in Nashville which had included the entire Negro population.

"I, Andrew Johnson, hereby proclaim freedom, full, broad and unconditional, to every man in Tennessee. This damnable aristocracy should be pulled down. No longer should the wives and daughters of the colored men of Tennessee be dragged into a concubinage compared to which polygamy is a virtue." He was the only southern senator who had not defected to the Confederacy. He never failed to speak with passion against the South. In 1862, Lincoln had sent him as military governor of Tennessee. His courage had restored Tennessee to the Union. As a reward for his lonely services and as a symbol of unity, he had been chosen Vice-President in 1864.

Harper's Magazine had written of him at that time, "There is no man in the country unless it be Mr. Lincoln himself whom the rebels more cordially hate. He fought them in the Senate when they counted upon his aid, and he has fought them steadily ever since."

The assassination brought shock and weeping, and some of the truest lamentations rose from the South, as Lincoln had offered goodwill; and goodwill is a powerful promise. Nothing you can put your finger on sometimes, but you trust it to grow into a fact.

Mingled with these true lamentations was a deep fear. White Southerners had always dreaded slave uprisings: there had been over three hundred, large and small, in the two hundred years of slavery.

On the Sunday morning after the assassination, General Eaton heard twice from the Commanding General that the surrounding countryside was terrified of an uprising to avenge the death of Lincoln. Each time Eaton sent back reassurance. But when a third message came, repeating the alarm and promising to hold him responsible for any disaster, he mounted his horse and rode to the Negro church, that immemorial incubator of freedom. He found such weeping that no one in the church saw him for some time. Later he went to the shacks and shanties. There he could not move because of importunate hands, holding, pulling him, to be reassured that slavery would not come again. He promised.

General Eaton was an honorable man. He had answered them out of his innocence. But slowly, inexorably, another question had to be answered by men more sophisticated than General Eaton: Who were the victors? The eleven million marginal whites were neither defeated nor victorious; they were just as anxious to get on with the future as any Northerner. The Negroes were clogging the roads ready to go in whatever direction freedom was found, just hoping no one would mistake them for runaway property.

Both were willing to say good-bye to the past, let the Yanks call it what they liked.

The master, the oligarch, had only his uniform without buttons, his pride, his antique determination that no past would be yielded, no concession made. Was this still, hard core from which power had sprung, the victor after all?

He rode the horse Grant had allowed him to keep and

18

while the dust was still settling on the roads he made his plans. *All that the oligarchy owned was land and a people. Much of the land might be exhausted by cotton but there were still millions of acres with which to fight the encroachment of industry and railroads, and millions of black fellows to make the fields golden and millions of whites to take orders from above.*

These old-fashioned men, sick in their pride, laid snares for the present. *We lost the war but we're undefeated and we need every last black and white fellow to cancel the day at Appomattox.*

When the war ended, these old-fashioned men remained out of power for about six weeks. Six weeks was all.

☆ 2 ☆

══════

FOR the men of the oligarchy, control of cheap southern labor was absolutely imperative. It was even more important in May 1865 than it had been in May 1860. Their political as well as agricultural recovery would have to be based on this iron control.

The Confederates knew that in their four years' absence from Congress, the congressional representation in the North had increased with all the vast new westward land. But they held an ace. In the past the slave had represented three-fifths of a man in the congressional count—though of course with no vote. Now, for better or worse, he would become a whole digit, and that digit would be controlled. It was as simple as that to the Confederates about to be a part of the Union again. When they sat once more in the empty seats they would speak for four million whole Negroes and that was impressive in any man's terms.

Say over and over: "Poor ignorant debased black fellow without a grain of common sense, incapable of self-government even if taught the rudiments of reading and writing, crying out for the experience and firm kindness of those who have ruled him for two hundred years . . ." It was an immensely strengthening rhetoric because it required reflex, not reflection.

Andrew Johnson of Tennessee, the new President, was one of the eleven million who had felt the iron hand of the oligarchy. He had been made Vice-President as a harmonizing gesture of unification, but men who really looked for harmony now considered him with alarm. To him, secession was treason and treason a crime which must be punished in the extreme. He was an emotionally splintered man, with a high voice and a steeltrap mouth, made bitter by the division within himself—half-slave, half-free in his attitude toward the southern aristocrat. "If Johnson were a snake," said Isham G. Harris, a Tennessee political rival, "he would lie in the grass and bite the heels of the rich men's children."

In public life he was given to wild extemporaneous speeches, but at one time he had written, "Gladly I would lay down my life if I could so engraft democracy into our general government that it would be permanent." He said, "The great plantations must be seized and divided into small farms."

He saw danger from two directions: "The aristocracy based on $3,000,000,000 of property in slaves . . . has disappeared but an aristocracy based on over $2,500,-000,000 of national securities has arisen in the northern states to assume that political control which the consolidation of great financial and political interests formerly gave to the slave oligarchy." He would fight both ways, but most he hated the slave oligarchs.

Ben Wade, the fierce antislavery senator from Ohio, said to him after he had been sworn in as President, "Mr. Johnson, I thank God that you are here. Lincoln had too much of the milk of human kindness to deal with these damned rebels. Now they will be dealt with according to their deserts."

He became President six days after Appomattox. Two weeks later he sent Chief Justice Salmon P. Chase, an opulent, reassuring figure, an antislavery worker in his youth, into the South to appraise the situation.

Charles Sumner, writing to an English friend, said, "The Chief Justice started yesterday on a visit to North Carolina, South Carolina, Florida and New Orleans. I anticipate much from this journey . . . I should not be surprised if we had this great question [justice for the Negroes] settled before the next meeting of Congress . . . With the President as well disposed as he shows himself to be, and the Chief Justice as positive, we shall prevail."

Sumner went on to quote Johnson, "Colored persons are to have the right of suffrage . . . the rebel states must go through a term of probation. The Chief Justice is authorized to say what the President desires and to do everything he can to promote organization without distinction of color. The President desires that the movement should appear to proceed from the people . . . I told him that while I doubted if the work could be effectively done without federal authority, I should be content provided equality before the law was secured for all without distinction of color. I said the rebel states could not come back except on the footing of the Declaration of Independence and the complete recognition of human rights. I feel more than ever confident that this will be fulfilled."

But Sumner cast a mighty shadow even on Presidents, and sometimes this got in his way. There were small confusing signs that no one wished to consider too hastily. In April, Tennessee had voted down a bill giving the vote to Negro and white men; the right to vote was confined to the white. Why did Johnson not make his power felt in his own state? He answered that if he were home he would take a stand, but look where he was. Disquieting word was coming from Mississippi, Georgia, North Carolina. Everyone seemed to know about this but Johnson. Thaddeus Stevens was sufficiently alarmed to call a caucus at the National Hotel in Washington on May 12. Both Wade and Sumner reassured the caucus. True, one must keep matters steady, but the President was safe, Negro suffrage would follow.

Chase, in South Carolina, found that the Southern Unionists—those white men anxious to heal old wounds and get on with life who were called "scalawags"—felt that their greatest hope for a new society lay in votes for the Negroes. These men were scattered all over the South, remarkable men, prosperous from railroads or small home industries, hating slavery, with a solid place in society and acutely aware of their moral responsibility to a democratic future. "All seemed embarrassed about first steps," Chase wrote to Johnson, "I am anxious that *you* should have the lead in this work. Nothing will so strengthen you with the people or bring such honor to your name throughout the world . . ."

Delay was really the only sin. It was a sin against a ravished land and its people, black and white. There were men of goodwill in every town and village; they must be strengthened. For four years the white Unionists had kept the Confederacy split and off balance. For four years a million black refugees had refused to work for their masters, had raised several million dollars' worth of cotton for a man they had never seen, Uncle Sam. Now they wanted peace, political power, and land.

Land needed the vote to hold it. In the southeast section of South Carolina, held by the Union forces since 1862, a convention had been called in April 1864 to elect delegates to the Presidential convention. Southern Union men were trying to get back into the Union, and these Union men invited all South Carolina men who shared their feelings. Two hundred and fifty came, and one hundred and fifty of them were Negroes. In this powerful stronghold of slavery, the convention had sounded like a shrill reveille.

What Chase saw—and Carl Schurz, the liberal senator from Wisconsin who followed him that spring—was incontrovertible. They saw a slowly breathing conquered land . . . suffering which spared neither man nor beast . . . a countryside that "looked for many miles like a broad black streak of ruin and desolation," (as Schurz said), "the fences all gone; lonesome smokestacks surrounded by dark heaps of ashes and cinders marking the spots where human habitation had stood; the fields along the road wildly overgrown by weeds, with here and there a sickly patch of cotton or corn cultivated by Negro squatters"—squatters demanding their patch of land.

But earth scorched by the Confederates or fought over by two armies was only a part of the picture. The war had roared up and down the waterways, the coast, but inside Alabama, Mississippi, Louisiana, Florida, very little change had taken place. Old power remained, with its roots as deep and tangled as an old tree's. "Many slaves had been removed by their masters as our armies penetrated the country," Schurz wrote. (He was going farther and seeing much more than Chase.) They were carried off "either to Texas or to the interior of Georgia and Alabama." There the masters could obscure, befuddle the end of slavery or "terrorize into submission. The white people were afraid of the Negroes and the Negroes did not trust the white people."

As Schurz and Chase bumped along the rutty roads, men, women, and children were coming in daily from these backways. They walked fifty, seventy miles to catch hold of a rumor. Freedom—freedom! Josh or Vash or Joe would get his bitty scrap of land? He'd ketch a learning? He'd be a man? He'd never go back home no more unless it was to measure the land. Suddenly Joe or Vash found he owned legs to carry him to Paradise if he could run that far.

The new men and women, without a cent to their names, were so rich in hope that they refused to put a hand to another man's plow. They glutted the roads which were already glutted with spring. Military posts had the appearance of great camp meetings.

The dust on the roads never settled. For there were also thousands of Confederate soldiers, some wounded, most hungry, struggling to get back to Alabama or Mississippi or—*sweet Jesus, maybe I'll just set down here and wait a spell till the world stops spinning.*

These soldiers could not go back any more than the black folks could, but where could they go *forward?* The men who had ruled them almost as absolutely as they had ruled the slaves, had lost the war. In all the din and bloody business something had been broken. Why should one take the time to mend it since it promised so little? Jeff Davis, rumor said, had tried to escape dressed as a woman.

The Negro was glutting the road for land, education, the vote. He did not trust a living soul unless he helped him to these promises. As far as the Negro was concerned, only certain kinds of men could be relied on in this promise-market. Only men like Chase and Schurz, only men like the agents of the new Freedmen's Bureau (which had grown out of Eaton's work), only Union soldiers, preferably black—talking of freedom at southern crossroads as though it were a fact—could be relied on to safeguard the future. They were all angels from Washington, that golden city, that new Jerusalem.

Suddenly, as improbable as thunder from a blue sky, a message broke promise and euphoria. On May 29, after six weeks of liberalism, Johnson announced a policy of

24

Confederate amnesty so sweeping that the Negro was left naked to the world. This amnesty offered free admission into citizenship for all white Southerners who would take an oath of loyalty to the Union. The only exceptions were officials of the Confederate government or officers above the rank of colonel or men worth $20,000 or more.

The shock was deep. The shock lay in the fact that Johnson's amnesty hardly differed from Lincoln's proposal but took a step backward: the President assumed all the prerogatives of pardon. By special application to him, men even in the excepted classifications could make themselves eligible for full citizenship. A bona fide citizen could then establish title to his land. A bona fide citizen could hold whatever public office he chose.

The Radical Republicans were appalled. Not only was the amnesty an old familiar bugbear to them (one they had thought moribund), but Johnson had acted as Lincoln would never have done—he had moved without Congress. Even if Lincoln had gained congressional approval for his amnesty, he would have put good men in key spots, North and South, and listened to what they said.

Johnson had moved without consultation with any congressional leader. Sumner, who had stuck like a burr to him all through the month of May, had not had a ghost of a hint. Johnson had acted like a conjuror and now presented himself as both magician and jinn. One conclusion seemed inescapable, that he wished to present an adjourned Congress with a display of personal power greater than any ever shown before by an elected official. "He will be crowned king before Congress meets," Sumner sent out the alarmed cry.

What had happened?

Schurz believed that William Seward, the Secretary of State, was Johnson's evil genius—as he had been Lincoln's evil genius in the opinion of those men who had fought all Seward's efforts to weaken the antislavery nature of the war. Thaddeus Stevens said sadly, "Seward entered into [Johnson] and ever since they have been running down steep places into the sea."

But the answer was also found in Johnson's complexity, the psychological malformation induced by his relation with the slave oligarchy. Despised in the past, he was now flattered by convocations of southern ladies and gentlemen who had begun to descend on the White House in April of 1865. They had assured him of his statesmanship; subtly but firmly they linked his new great destiny with theirs. Southerners all. The pressure became almost incalculable.

May, June, July it increased. Everyone talked about it. In midsummer, Schurz tried to see Johnson. He had his carpetbag filled with the proof that the President must abandon this course.

"Arriving at Washington I reported myself at once to the White House. The President's secretary . . . announced me to the President who sent out word he was busy . . . I called again the next morning. The President was still busy. I asked the secretary to submit to the President that I had returned from a journey made at the President's personal request . . . [The President then] received me without a smile of welcome . . . He said I need not write out a general report on his account. I replied that I considered it a duty. The President did not answer. The silence became awkward and I bowed myself out.

"President Johnson evidently wished to suppress the testimony as to the conditions of things in the South. I resolved not to let him do so . . . Among my friends in Washington were different opinions as to how the striking change in [his] attitude had been brought about. Some told me that the White House had been fairly besieged by southern men and women of high social standing who had told the President that the only element of trouble in the south consisted of a lot of fanatical abolitionists who excited the Negroes with all sorts of dangerous notions and that all would be well if he could only restore the southern state governments as quickly as possible . . . and that he was a great man to whom they looked up as a saviour. Now it was thought that Mr. Johnson, who before the war was treated with undisguised contempt by the slaveholding aristocracy, could not withstand the subtle flattery of the same aristocracy when they flocked around him as humble suppliants cajoling his vanity."

Though Congress had adjourned in March and would not reassemble until December, Radical Republicans kept their dismay vibrant. "The consent of the governed," was the cry Sumner raised and he made clear that the "governed" in a republic were all citizens irrespective of color.

It was a situation without precedent any place in the world.

At the dead center was the South moldering in the summer sun.

* 3 *
=====

THE SOUTH needed capital. It needed farm machinery which had been virtually unknown in a land where human muscles were cheaper than harrows. Northern looms and spindles had been starved for four years, and there was cash and credit waiting for cotton. When northern mill owners and factory owners came bustling down the southern roads, blueprints in their carpetbags, a welcome shone in most eyes. These men were healthy specimens and they brought a healthy promise. They looked about and they invested their capital. The labor market was good. They bid accordingly. They bought homes or left their agents to guard against any mischance. They were offering wages so low that no white man would accept them—only black men who were not accustomed to wages. Yet the offers jerked from the planters' cries of outrage. Wages meant a social revolution undermining every plan they had for the future. They could not meet these wages and did not propose to try. They proposed to control the labor and, by the labor, the vote. Let the busy little men from the North beware if they tried to shift the base of power. Samson had brought down a temple for less than that!

But within a few months of the war's end, a syndicate of Northerners had made a wide sweep of investments from plantations to railroads. The South had plenty of plantations, very few railroads. Speculators knew that the plantations—or rather their systems—had to be controlled in order to make the railroads a fact.

In North Carolina, turpentine and lumber offered a rich harvest.

Union soldiers were being demobilized as fast as practical, but the remaining regiments would be needed a while longer to make sure that both wages and investments had a chance to take root.

. . . Political power became an obsession with the planter. From Virginia to Texas, national banks were attempting to control the postwar inflation. This required northern johnnies-on-the-spot, for Southerners, since the days of Jackson, had done all they could to let the stuffings out of centralized banks and their efforts had not altered. . . . Nor had their refrain *All that will save the old South is planter political power!*

The poor whites accepted gladly whatever opportunities were offered by planter or by northern investor, for they had few dreams. But the Negro was different. He had a dream, and he did not trust any one but that northern gentleman, Mr. Government Power.

All through the long hot summer, the Negro waited. He went hungry; he farmed his patch if he had it; he listened, talked, waited. He waited because he was afraid if he put his mark to any work contract he would sell himself back into slavery and that would put the final quietus on his dream. He also waited because he was bathed in the afflatus of the dream that he would own land.

This dream was like a perpetual sun. If the sun seemed to go down, it was brought up again by the Union soldier, Negro, who nine times out of ten had been a slave like himself and could reassure him that the world was his if he took it.

These Negro soldiers were remarkable human beings. They had learned the blazing facts of freedom by running away from slavery or by joining the Union armies at recruiting stations or in the field. General Eaton told of one occasion in Tennessee when the chaplain "painted the terrors and duties of war as black and as stern as his imagination could conjure them, and finished by asking those who were ready to face these dangers to move out one step from the line. The whole line swept toward him as one man."

Afraid of no one, it seemed, fighters in an old Gideon sense, blazing hot with their proven knowledge, they said land gave security; the vote held it; education explained it all. Education was perpetual fruit on the tree. Education was a bucket always filled with fresh water when the days grew hot.

During the spring and summer of 1865, schools sprouted like crabgrass. All the work done in the Valley of the Mississippi, in Louisiana, in South Carolina by the Department of Freedmen was continued as urgently as ever. The Freedmen's Bureau had been shaped out of the old Department for this purpose as much as anything else —(and we will come to that story in just a moment). The Bureau depended on church volunteers just as it had during the war, and the volunteers came with the same readiness. Eager young Presbyterians, Methodists, Quakers hurried down the rickety roads. They were nice religious youngsters brimming with ideals or older teachers who loved learning or runaway slaves who had gotten an education in the North. Missionary and antislavery societies heard the call of a whole race trying to go to school. It was like the day of Pentecost, the descent of the spirit. "Few were too young and none too old to make the attempt to learn," Booker T. Washington said.

The Bureau did not have enough money to supply books, slates, pencils, or paper, but they did supply whatever protection they could. The shade of a tree or a church was the school. A Bible or a Farmer's Almanac was the first textbook. Learning was a great bright light and it transformed the whole world.

The wanderers, those who had been searching up and down for mother, father, husband, wife, sold away nine, ten years ago, God knows where, tended to settle if a school took root. Then *they* took root. They got married in the school, or under the tree. Sometimes old grayheads found each other again. A community became stabilized.

It was enough to drive an old-fashioned white person out of his head. Carl Schurz found only "a small minority" of whites aware of the fact that education could not be kept from the Negro. That "small minority" was willing to support private schools, "but whenever I asked whether it might be hoped that the legislature of their states or their county authorities would make provision for Negro education, I never received an affirmative and only in two or three instances feebly encouraging answers. At last I was forced to the conclusion, that aside from a small number of honorable exceptions, the popular prejudice is bitterly set . . . 'Negro education will be the ruin of the South.' "

The full implications of this spontaneous education have never been fully appreciated. It was the foundation of all public school education in the South—not only of the free unsegregated schools which would, within a few months, be authorized state by state by the Negro and white legislators, but also of the industrial schools and the colleges which alone, in the segregated wilderness that followed, would develop Negro teachers, clergymen, physicians.

It was against these teachers, these Freedmen's agents, that Johnson's aristocratic visitors were warning him all through the summer. And well they might, for these volunteers were accomplishing one of the greatest wonders in American history with faith as their only tool.

The Freedmen's Bureau—or correctly, the Bureau of Refugees, Freedmen and Abandoned Lands—was the first federal social agency in the United States, and it must have had the seal of divinity upon it if one judged from its miracles. To confirm the work of General Eaton in the Valley of the Mississippi, the work of General Banks in New Orleans, and of General Saxton in the Department of the South required something better than the awkward improvisations that the Senate and House had tossed back and forth to each other for two years. Antislavery congressmen were also afraid that if the white South was left as sole custodian of the Negro, an attempt would be made to reestablish a variation on slavery.

The final bill, shaping the new Bureau under the War Department, was knocked together with a few words and a blessing, and was signed by Lincoln in March 1865.

Perhaps its salvation lay in the fact it did not tempt bureaucrats. It was given no appropriation. Peripheral agencies of the government, concerned with the Negro, contributed to it, but most of its funds came from the rents paid into it by the Negro squatters who leased abandoned lands.

Johnson appointed General Oliver O. Howard as its head. He was perhaps the Bureau's greatest single asset. Thirty-five years old, born in Maine, with one arm lost in the war, he was a man remarkable for his compassion and his inability to distinguish color.

In May, assistant commissioners of the old Department of Freedmen had hurriedly gathered in Washington and agreed upon the divisions of labor. (Eaton was called from Tennessee to take charge of the District of Columbia, Virginia, and Maryland.) Headquarters were established in twelve southern states. General Howard gave them one directive: get to work.

Starvation and suffering must be averted. The philosophy of the Bureau dictated that work and self-respect would be the quickest way to cut down on the suffering. The assistant commissioners knew the rules by heart:

". . . Simple good faith, for which we hope on all hands from those concerned in the passing away of slavery, will especially relieve the Assistant Commissioners in the discharge of their duties toward the freedmen. The Assistant Commissioners will everywhere declare and protect their freedom as set forth by the Proclamation of the President and the laws of Congress . . .

"Loyal refugees who have been driven from their homes will, on their return, be protected from abuse, and the calamities of their situation relieved as much as possible . . .

"Negroes must be free to choose their own employers and be paid for their labor. Agreements must be free, bonafide acts, and their inviolability enforced on both parties. The old system of overseers, tending to compulsory unpaid labor and acts of cruelty and oppression, is prohibited.

"The unity of families and all the rights of the family relationship will be carefully guarded. In places where the local statutes make no provision for the marriage of people of color, the Assistant Commissioners are authorized to designate an officer who shall keep a record of marriages which may be solemnized by an ordained minister of the gospel. Registrations will be carefully preserved . . .

"Assistant Commissioners will aid refugees and freedmen in securing titles to land according to law. This may be done for them as individuals or by encouraging joint stock companies."

Recruiting of agents went on continually. Anyone who was devoted enough to initiate the freedmen into the experience of citizenship was wanted. Many Negroes were among the agents. They were either northern Negroes or former slaves who had escaped to the North, gotten an education, and now returned to put it to use.

The thin line of federal troops deployed over the South —nine thousand in all—were their only protection. Crises were met as they arose. Hope-for-the-best was often the loftiest philosophy that could be summoned, and improvisation became a way of life.

The Assistant Commissioners and their agents had a fighting opponent on their hands from the start: the planter. The planter would not stand for three things: federal interference with labor, firearms in the hands of the Negro and a vote in his pocket.

The Bureau had been given life for only one year. In that year it must defeat or persuade the planter and make over an entire social system by "simple good faith."

It had almost unlimited authority but few ways to enforce it. The Bureau knew better than any that the whole burden of adjustment must not fall on the South. The entire country bore the guilt of slavery and must bear the responsibility for freedom. "The sudden collapse of the rebellion, making emancipation an actual universal fact, was like an earthquake," General Howard wrote years later. "Even well-disposed and humane landowners were at a loss what to do or how to begin the work of reorganizing society."

The Bureau knew that unless the landless Southerner, Negro or white, was given his footing, chaos would follow. The Bureau sought out the "well-disposed humane landowners" and valiantly fought for contracts at stipulated wages. And then valiantly fought the Negroes to sign

them. Here and there Negroes signed, but most would not
. . . How did a man know he was not signing himself back
into slavery? Where was that little scrap of land that was
to be his own? (In many places dishonest men did a flour-
ishing business selling red, white, and blue stakes at $2.00
apiece. *Confirm your claim! Stake it in red, white and
blue!*)

The agents explained and scolded. Contracts insured a
cash crop. They were sacred. The white man would have
to live up to them as much as the freedman. Some of you
think if you put your mark on a contract you will somehow be made a slave. This is a lie, there is no danger. It is
also a lie that you will be branded when you get on a
plantation. *Do not be afraid, do not be afraid, do not be
afraid.*

A regiment of Negro soldiers from Louisiana saved its
pay till $50,000 had been accumulated. All that summer
they negotiated for five large plantations which they
could turn into villages. (More Negro soldiers came from
Louisiana than any other state: twenty-four thousand.)
A regiment had numerical power. But planters made one
fact perfectly clear: they would fight another war if necessary to keep labor dependent, the Negroes without land.

The Bureau brought landowners into court. Or, standing in the middle of a field, agents adjudicated like simple
Solomons. "Scarcely any subject that had to be legislated
upon in civil society," Howard wrote, "failed at one time
or another to demand the action of this singular bureau."
It brought medical aid to one million freedmen. With fourteen surgeons and three assistant surgeons (and such local
volunteers as they could get) the Negro death rate was cut
from 30 percent to 13 percent in that year. (By 1869 it
had been cut to 2.03 percent.) The blind, the deaf, the
insane, the aged, the orphaned were all cared for. The
Bureau established hospitals where none had ever existed.
It gave out over twenty-one million rations, many to
poverty-stricken whites.

Concern was its motive. Compassion made it work.

It was hated by the white planter with a venom that charged it with every sin in the world.

All that summer northern industry cast a benign effusion over the South. Northern industry promised to make the rough places plain, give manliness to the Negro, prosperity to the white, and be a greater source of union than any government intrusion into states' affairs.

It was Johnson's reconstruction which provided a grotesque and cruel impasse.

He had issued his Declaration of Amnesty on May 29. Within three days, Provisional Governors had been appointed for North Carolina and Mississippi. In June, Georgia, Texas, Alabama, and South Carolina had been provided with governors, and Florida, in July. They were all experienced, old-line white politicians from their own states. The genuine Unionists who were willing to stand up and be counted as friends of the landless whites and friends of the Negro were abruptly passed over. These Union men lived through a nightmare of disillusionment and physical violence.

In addition Johnson recognized the "ten-per-cent" governments of Louisiana, Arkansas, and Tennessee. By midsummer Texas remained the only Confederate state. (The confusion there was too great for any civilian authority to have a chance of survival.)

Johnson was using all his prerogatives in order to present Congress with accomplished facts when it convened in December 1865. His Presidential pardons were for anyone's asking. In order to speed the clemency petitions, he appointed M. F. Pleasants, a former Confederate colonel, as clerk of pardons.

"Pardoning became a big business with lawyers and brokers promising clients pardons for fees ranging from $150 to $500. This was an ideal climate for corruption, for the enormous pressure applied by those who wanted pardons in order to participate in political activities or to reclaim their property made graft inevitable . . . By September [pardons] were being granted at the rate of more than one hundred a day," says John Hope Franklin in *Reconstruction After the Civil War*.

The white Southerners, who had been hostile to the Confederacy, and the Negro were suddenly at the mercy of ghosts from the past.

"Regulators" began to appear. Some were Confederate soldiers, dislocated and restless, some were youths, idle and looking for trouble, but their "mission," according to the *New York Herald* which no one could call pro-Negro, "is to visit summary justice upon any offenders against the public peace. It is needless to say that their attention is largely directed to maintaining quiet and submission among the blacks. The shooting or stringing up of some obstreperous 'nigger' by the 'regulators' is so common an occurrence as to excite little remark. Nor is the work of proscription confined to the freedmen. The 'regulators' go to the bottom of the matter and strive to make it uncomfortably warm for any new settler with demoralizing innovations of wages for 'niggers.' "

Southerners of goodwill were disturbed but they did not know what to do. They stressed the terrible upheaval that came at the end of a war. But men with a more staunch realism saw that within three months of President Lincoln's assassination, the old masters were in power again.

Negro soldiers counseled retaliation. All that summer Johnson was bombarbed with demands to get the Negro soldiers out of the South. They looked and acted too much like men. The life of a Negro soldier was not worth a bent pin if he were found alone on a road.

General Grant was sent down for a short swing around, and he echoed the pleas for his hosts. He pointed out that since the Negro soldiers had themselves been slaves, they "demoralize labor both by their advice and by furnishing in their camps" a place for the freedmen to gather. He urged that only white troops be stationed in the South.

Florida had a large concentration of Negro soldiers. A friend wrote to Johnson from Tallahassee, "There is really danger of an insurrection that would surprise you if you were aware of it, raised principally from the secret administration of colored troops."

Schurz had reported the opposite side of the story. "Armed bands of white men patrol the country roads to drive back the wandering Negro." Bodies of murdered Negroes were often found at dawn by the roadside. "Gruesome reports came from the hospitals—reports of colored men and women whose ears had been cut off, whose skulls had been broken by blows, whose bodies had been slashed by knives or lacerated with scourges. A number of such cases I examined myself. A veritable reign of terror prevails in many parts of the South."

Vagrancy laws began to bristle in every state. Any black man on the road became a vagrant. Field hands, laying down their tools to sing or dance, became vagrants, Negro soldiers, mustered out only a few hours, were often seized as vagrants.

Union League and Republican party meetings were attacked, in Mississippi, by virtue of an old law which made vagrants out of those who were "found unlawfully assembling together, either in the day or night-time," and teachers and Freedmen's Bureau agents were transformed into vagrants when they "associated with free Negroes or mulattoes." Curfew laws became a special form of harassment, for any Negro without a pass was liable to arrest.

To harass the Union Leagues was to show an inverted wisdom. They were centers for voter education.

As early as May, Chief Justice Chase had written Johnson, "Everywhere, throughout the country, colored citizens

37

are organizing Union Leagues." He told Johnson that the Leagues would soon represent "a power which no wise statesman will despise."

During the war Union Leagues had been formed in New York, Philadelphia, and Boston by white Republicans. They had represented a militant patriotic support of the war, were strongly antislavery. They had mobilized support and supplies for Union troops, enlisted Negroes, worked with the Department of Freedmen caring for the slaves in refugee camps and assisting the poorer groups of whites in the southern states occupied by the Union armies.

With the end of the war, the northern Leagues had become gentlemen's clubs and, in time, archconservative. But in the South they were the bailiwicks of social change. White men—scalawags, Union soldiers, teachers— belonged to them also. Classes were given, simple pamphlets were written explaining issues. Negro soldiers, demobilized, joined the Leagues and by virtue of the guns they retained, helped the Leagues to form voluntary militia—stockades, as it were, in a bitter wilderness. White and Negro drilled together.

Women formed auxiliaries.

The Leagues provided an answer to the growing terror, for they stressed independence and self-respect. *Don't be afraid!*

All summer the confusion ran deep and wide. Congressmen, sitting at home, were angry and impotent. They were determined to have the last word but events were moving so fast that the last word became a race for a new word tomorrow.

By Presidential order, constitutional conventions were ordered in Mississippi, Alabama, South Carolina, North Carolina, Georgia, and Florida to repeal the secession ordinances, ratify the Thirteenth Amendment abolishing slavery, and draw up new constitutions. When these requirements had been fulfilled, Southern governors, senators and representatives could be elected.

Leaders of the Confederacy had returned to positions of power so rapidly that they took over the election of delegates to the conventions. Southern Unionists were systematically passed over in favor of men who were recipients of Presidential patronage.

Not a word was said about Negro participation. The delegates would be white men elected by white men, with no further restrictions.

But since equal suffrage divided even the Radical Republicans—Was the Negro ready? Should not education come first and then an elite sample of voters?—this absolute silence on Negro voters alarmed only men like Stevens and Sumner.

All through the hot months, Sumner, with his obsessive belief that freedom was Christian and indivisible, discussed nothing else. He talked about the rights of Negroes on the street, at dinner parties, in society wherever he went. He implored the members of the Cabinet not to follow Seward's divisive lead. Four of them were, he knew, terribly uneasy about developments but had taken no action.

To Sumner politics was a matter of morality. He wrote tirelessly about Negro rights. He had his speeches copied and distributed like throwaways. He made the issue a simple one: Who had won the Civil War? The slave masters or the free North?

Abolitionists like Wendell Phillips and Frederick Douglass, who had brought to the freedom fight a broad base of social and economic thinking, were making speech after speech to large crowds of white men and Negroes. They stressed the emotional dangers that came with relaxation at the end of a war, they warned against a false confidence that the Thirteenth Amendment had taken care of all problems. Too many sensible men had thrown their hats into the air and considered that the day had been won.

Phillips' and Douglass' speeches were also printed. George Stearns, an antislavery business man of Boston, raised $50,000 to fight complacency. He sent out one hundred thousand copies of newspapers carrying the speeches and fifty thousand pamphlets. He printed forty thousand copies of an especially strong speech by Sumner.

"I thought I had made my last antislavery speech," Sumner said in Massachusetts in the fall of 1865. "I was mistaken . . . neither the rebellion nor slavery is yet ended . . . Slavery has been abolished in name, that is all. It is essential that all men be hailed as equal before the law; and this enfranchisement must be both political and civil."

He did not trust the old leaders of the South, but he said, "I would not be harsh. There is nothing humane that I would reject. Nothing in hate. Nothing in vengeance. I am for a velvet glove, but for a while I wish the hand of iron."

Thaddeus Stevens was holding his heaviest fire. Stevens was an enormously skillful politician who saw politics as the servant of man, and man he saw man-high. He held his fire because he knew one factor was not yet in line: the North. As long as common opinion in the North still wondered whether the Negro was a man or whether it was right to raise a new class of laborers into a voting force, there was great work still to be done.

On August 14, 1865, Mississippi held the first of the constitutional conventions. The convention conceded that slavery was over, but fought every other concession to the Negro. This included the owning and renting of land.

The Negro Mississippians met to tell Congress their fears of reenslavement. Johnson wrote in some haste to Provisional Governor William Sharkey, urging that Negroes with education be given the vote as this "would completely disarm the adversary" in Congress. The suggestion did not receive any attention whatever. The government of Mississippi was defined: it was a "white man's government." But the *Columbus Sentinel* was sure it spoke for many realistic Mississippians when it called the legislators "as complete a set of political Goths as were ever turned loose to work destruction upon a state. The fortunes of the whole South have been injured by their folly."

In Boston Wendell Phillips said, "Our philosophy of government since the fourth day of July, 1776, is that no class is safe, no freedom is real, no emancipation is effectual which does not place in the hands of the man himself the power to protect his own rights. This is the genius of American institutions."

If northern business could be persuaded that Negro enfranchisement would be to its advantage, the situation could be almost controlled. *Votes for the Negro. Enfranchise the black man. Bind him to the Republican party.* It did not much matter how it was phrased, but *give him the vote* . . . Give it *back* to him was an even more correct way of putting it, for many free Negroes had voted in the eighteenth century, and their final disfranchisement had not taken place until 1835—within a young man's memory.

State by state the southern conventions were held, setting up the machinery for elections immediately afterward. The Thirteenth Amendment had been adopted in all of the seceded states except Mississippi. North Carolina had attached reservations to her adoption, and Georgia retained the right to ask compensation for her freed slaves, but Johnson was satisfied that his requirements were being met.

Because Mississippi had rejected the Thirteenth Amendment, Mississippi was a terrible awkwardness to him. And Louisiana, where a government had already been recognized, was in a state of such shocking upheaval that the Democrats were in complete control of the state and had adopted a platform at their state convention which declared Louisiana "a government of white people, made and to be perpetuated for the exclusive political benefit of the white race." But Johnson had to claim his tiger was subdued even while he clung to its tail.

Not a single convention had seriously discussed the possibility of Negro suffrage. As the new constitutions were announced, state by state, the pattern became unmistakably clear: the Negro must be held in a grip trained and conditioned by the past.

The only genuflection to the change brought by the war was in the relations of white men to each other. In the South Carolina convention, nonslaveholding whites had forced an end to the parish system which had always insured that the planters would control the state government. They had forced other reforms as well, such as an end to property qualifications, but they refused to count Negroes as a basis of apportionment.

The relations between planters and nonslaveholding whites had always been hostile and uneasy. In the past the nonslaveholder had been sucked into a powerful machine by virtue of his white skin, not by virtue of a common interest. The monopoly of land by the planter, the degradation implied by white labor, had created a stigma of inferiority. These conventions—and the legislatures that followed—became a curious dream-like struggle between white men which removed the stigma only by slamming the door more violently against the black man.

This process took several weeks. First the conventions fulfilled Johnson's requirements; then elections were held for state and congressional officers; finally the legislatures met.

During those summer and autumn weeks the massive intention became perfectly clear; white men's governments were being formed, entrenched, buttressed, and rendered impregnable.

The Negro was given nothing.

Education was voted on, state by state, for all but the Negro. Free schools at public expense had "as the sole aim

. . . to educate every white child in the commonwealth." Florida conceded that Negroes might want to learn, but for this privilege they would have to pay a special tax.

In court a Negro's word could not be accepted over a white man's.

For many types of work the Negro could not work without a license; fees ranged from ten to one hundred dollars. Travel across state lines became almost impossible.

The Negro could rent only in restricted areas. He could never be without his license from the police or his contract of labor. If he quit his work he could be arrested and sent to a house of correction for a year; his captor would be repaid five dollars plus ten cents a mile for travel.

No Negro, unless a soldier, could own or carry arms. For "seditious speeches, insulting gestures, language or acts," he could be fined and imprisoned. In order to leave no doubt of the law's intention, Mississippi stated simply that the old regulations controlling slavery were fully operative again except "so far as the mode and manner of trial and imprisonment have been changed and altered by law."

In every state an employer could hold over a Negro a power as arbitrary as a slavemaster's, and could "re-enslave" the Negro's children by apprenticeship laws.

This led many to conclude that wages and contracts were the heresies being anathematized by these laws.

The laws permitted the Negro no freedom in his new life save legal marriage, the right to hold property, the right to sue or be sued.

The Freedmen's Bureau raised the alarm. In several states the Assistant Commissioners ordered the Black Codes (as they were called) repealed, or the Bureau agents rescinded their enforcement. Union soldiers were occasionally called on for a display of arms—which of course brought cries of tyranny.

The alarm of the Negroes was profound. They held

43

mass meetings in Norfolk, Richmond, and Petersburg, Virginia; in Vicksburg and in Jackson, Mississippi; in Nashville, Tennessee; in Raleigh, North Carolina, and Charleston, South Carolina. They demanded equal rights and the ballot—and land.

In Nashville a local barber was chairman. Resolutions demanded that Congress recognize the rights of Negro citizenship in precisely the same way it had "recognized the rights and humanity of the black man" when it had ordered Negro regiments to be formed "to save the Union." And it questioned the propriety of seating Tennessee congressmen until the state recognized the rights of Negroes.

In North Carolina the chairman was a former slave named John Harris, who for years had been partaking of a secret education. The North Carolina convention took special notice of the fact that John S. Rock, a Boston Negro, had been admitted to practice law before the Supreme Court in February of that year. The meeting also pledged support to friends—and they named the friends they most trusted—Thaddeus Stevens and Charles Sumner.

In November, South Carolina Negroes met to protest the new-old consititution. Free education was essential to a democracy—it belonged to every child, colored as well as white. "Every citizen, without regard to race, descent or color should have equal political rights." Some extraordinary men directed this convention.

Martin J. Delany, for example, of a free Negro family, had gotten not only an adequate education, but had graduated from the Harvard Medical School as a doctor. In the last days of the war he had been commissioned a major. Richard H. Cain, also a free Negro, had gone to college in Ohio, become active in the Methodist church, and in time would become a bishop. J. J. Wright, a northern Negro, had been admitted to the Pennsylvania bar. Beverly Nash had been born and raised a slave but was busy making up for lost time.

The memorials that they sent to Congress were written in Spencerian English, but the sentiments were the well-established attitudes of men desiring to be free. And an urgency pervaded the sentiments, for time was moving backward. Land, given to them, was being taken away.

Every Johnson pardon included an order to restore confiscated land. Planters, with their pardons in their pockets, were claiming their land. Negroes who had moved onto the fields and cultivated them did not have even the right of squatters.

But claiming the land and reoccupying it were often two different things. If Negro regiments were stationed near the plantation in dispute, a pitched battle might be fought. If Negro soldiers were not available, hoes and shovels held the enemy at bay for a time.

On the Sea Islands, the Negroes had by now built comfortable houses and schools and established communities. By every honorable promise, including that of Sherman himself, the land was theirs. When the planters appeared there, they were met by Negroes with pitchforks. Freedmen's agents refused to release the land, and sent urgent petitions to Congress to confirm promises made in wartime. But Congress was not in session.

In Charleston, General Howard was obliged to yield a large plantation. He was heartsick. Looking down at the worried dark faces, he did not know what to say. To give himself a moment to recover, he asked for a song. On the edge of the crowd, an old woman lifted her voice. "Nobody Knows de Trouble I've Seen." Howard wept.

Some of the Negroes did not give up even then. They drew up a badly spelled petition to the President saying how "sad" they felt over his decree and they begged for an acre and a half if he would not give them more. He did not reply.

By wintertime the old ways and old masters had laid a straight path across the South. Everywhere the Negroes

45

had been thrown back. But around them stood their allies like hastily constructed but sturdy fences—the teachers, the Union soldiers, the Freedmen's agents. The planters hated the Freedmen's agents most of all for they had legal power and they had used this power; they stood in the position the planters had expected to occupy, adviser and confidant.

The profits of northern business were still enormously high; vast amounts of capital were awaiting investment. By December, Johnson has given fourteen thousand pardons to men on the proscribed list, thus opening the way for business cooperation. But as one state after the other met his requirements by repealing the secession ordinances and ratifying the Thirteenth Amendment, he knew that a fight was just beginning. He had gotten what he believed was right—he saw himself as the god of national unity, white unity that is—but he was aware that congressmen were bristling with anger and suspicion, and that the Black Codes could undo all his work.

He quickly proclaimed the war at an end and civil governments in control of the seceded states. Congress would be confronted with accomplishments almost impossible to rescind.

"Hold the antislavery societies together," Sumner wrote to New England, "the crisis is grave . . . Nobody can tell certainly what pressure the President will bring to bear on Congress, and how Congress can stand it. I think that Congress will insist upon time—this will be our first demand."

Every congressman knew—and the Democrats best of all—that the Republicans were not a party of strength but of coalitions. All shades of opinion colored the party. Johnson's shrewdness dawned somewhat late on the more conservative. He was stealing their power, yet no one dared rock the boat, for the Radical Republicans were almost as alarming to the conservatives as was this

46

usurper of power. The Conservative Republicans hoped for the best.

Thaddeus Stevens prepared for the worst.

This extraordinary man, keener than a knife, with a tongue like a blade of steel, is the most controversial figure in American history. To his enemies he was a Robespierre. To the Negroes he was second only to Lincoln.

A French journalist writing from Washington as congressmen gathered in the fall of 1865 said that the second American revolution was about to begin.

☆ 4 ☆

═══════

JOHN VAN BUREN, son of the eighth President of the United States, said that fall in a speech in Albany, New York, that the Negro was "chiefly fit to black boots and cut hair."

The 39th Congress had many men who agreed with him.

It had also men who, though confused, were idealistic and eager to get into step with the present. When Thaddeus Stevens looked down the aisles of the House, his burning eyes under heavy brows took the measure of his colleagues. He knew them all. He had on his desk a sheaf of papers—reports and affidavits of intimidation, terror, and chaos. This was all the ammunition he needed. He was like an old flame which burned more brightly as it came toward its end. He was tired and sick, but he had not

47

spent his entire adult life fighting for the rights of human beings to cool his passion now.

There seemed no doubt about the temper of Congress. Conservative Republicans, Radical Republicans, and northern Democrats, all jealous of their constitutional authority, watched the President coldly.

In his annual message he announced that the requirements for a return to the Union had been met by every state but Mississippi and Texas, which had not yet been able to hold a convention. As to the elective franchise for the freedmen, that was a matter for the states to determine. He may have glanced toward the sixty-nine Southerners who had arrived with their credentials as duly elected representatives from the late Confederacy.

Alexander Stephens of Georgia, the former Vice-President of the Confederacy, four Confederate generals, six Confederate Cabinet members and fifty-eight members of the Confederate congress—all members of that category proscribed by both Lincoln and Johnson—were waiting to have their credentials accepted. Johnson had extended a pardon to all of them.

Congress proposed to exercise one of its powers without delay: the right to determine its own membership. Congress refused to recognize the credentials of the sixty-nine. By this act, Congress threw down its first challenge to the President. By that one act it raised the whole question of power and prerogative.

Stevens called a Republican caucus and submitted a plan for a Committee of Fifteen to be drawn from both Houses and both parties in Congress. As Dr. W. E. B. DuBois notes in *Black Reconstruction:* "It was the business of the Committee to see how the government of the United States was to be changed after war . . . and this involved first, some change in the basis of popular representation; secondly, a clarification of the status of the Negro; and finally, it brought a modification of the relation of the national government to state governments, not simply in civil rights but even more in industry and labor. It was through the first and second that the majority which eventually dominated the 39th Congress gained its moral power. It was through the third that the moral power was implemented."

Stevens was too astute not to stress practical matters first. By a curious irony, the Thirteenth Amendment, when it was ratified, would add twenty-nine representatives from the South. This was enough to dramatize the situation for northern congressmen.

Stevens set forth the principle that Reconstruction was the prerogative of Congress, that the President's actions were provisional and not binding on Congress. The committee itself would inquire into conditions in the "so-called Confederate States of America and report whether they, or any of them, are entitled to representation in either House of Congress."

Congress agreed and a Joint Committee of six senators and nine members of the House was appointed.

Business disquiet was immediately reported from New York. The *New York Herald* reported that commerce was especially uneasy lest Stevens carry through his plan for land confiscation. "Such wholesale confiscation, capital could not contemplate."

The day after Christmas, Stevens presented his first proposal. This was to base southern representation upon voters.

By "voters" there was no doubt he meant white *and* Negro.

In the Senate, Sumner had, on the first day of the session, presented his sheaf of bills and resolutions: equality "before the law whether in the courtroom or at the ballot box," Negro jurors on cases involving Negroes, enforcement of the amendment prohibiting slavery. He also offered a careful blueprint for Reconstruction, giving Congress authority to insure equality before the law and prevent discrimination by race or color. And he asked for equal suffrage in the District of Columbia.

This cut too close to the bone. A storm broke out. Johnson saw the District as an entering wedge leading "to a war between the races which would result in great injury to both and the certain extermination of the Negro population."

The Committee of Fifteen, groping its way, saw the reactions of Congress as a prism. Congress ruled the District; equality at the seat of government would be an irrevocable statement of national intent. It would leave no room for maneuver.

The passions and dangers of the next few months were only barely defined by the struggles in Congress. The Freedmen's Bureau, an anchor in this stormy sea, had to be made as safe as its insecure position allowed. A Civil Rights Bill, introduced into the Senate in December, had to be made as watertight as possible. These two measures did not seem to Stevens and Sumner, guiding policy, to be so controversial that they were in danger.

Trumbull of Illinois, a friend of Lincoln, was persuaded to introduce the Civil Rights Bill. The bill made it a criminal offense to deny on the basis of color any civil rights enjoyed by a white man.

This seemed a simple proposition, but the aisles exploded with protests. Senator John Sherman of Ohio, Republican, said there was not a state in the Union which did not have laws discriminating against a man because of his color. Such a bill was far too embarrassing . . . wait till the Thirteenth Amendment had been adopted.

The Radical Republicans were already on their way to a Fourteenth Amendment. They were convinced that only land, education, and the vote would ultimately resolve the problem for the new American voters. The Democrats saw more and more sharply that some version of the *status quo ante* must be confirmed and modernized in order to fight the danger of these new voters swarming into the Republican party.

"Any Democrat who did not hint in his speech that the Negro is a degenerate gorilla would be considered lacking in enthusiasm," wrote journalist Georges Clemençeau to his newspaper in Paris. "The idea of giving political power to a lot of wild men incapable of civilization, whose intelligence is no higher than that of the animals—this is the theme of all Democratic speeches."

The Democratic whip in the House, James Brooks of New York, found it appropriate to spend an hour insisting that the Negro was the physical inferior of the white man. At the end, Stevens rose and said briefly that "the immortal soul of the Negro has the same prerogatives of damnation or redemption as has Mr. Brooks'."

The pressures from all directions were formidable. Speeches on constitutional metaphysics reached such points of obscurity that only a ruthless mind could cut through the obfuscation. Stevens, in the House, tried to bring the debates back to two subjects: the basis of representation in Congress and the status of the Negro.

The Thirteenth Amendment was added to the Constitution late in December, but by then the Freedmen's Bureau bill was jostling the more windy defenders of constitutional iconolatry.

The most important single agency for law and progress in the South had an authority so poorly defined, so unsupported, that both its life and its power depended upon the most skillful juggling.

In many ways the Bureau demonstrated what was wrong with the whole business of the present and future. The only organized symbol of order and self-respect for southern Negroes—fighting for its life—its right to do the lonely job of making laws and interpreting them, acting as guardians and custodians, imposing and collecting taxes—it faced such perpetual congressional hostility that its continuation was a miracle. Moving with infinite caution, trying not to alienate local opinion to the point of an impasse, afflicted in some places with poor agents, obliged to suggest rather than demand positive actions, the Bureau was regarded by the South as a curse, a "foreign occupation," and by the North as deeply suspect.

Northern congressmen made it their football, protesting federal credit in any form, delivering orotund perorations against idleness and shiftless Negroes.

Stevens angrily pointed out that without capital or credit to buy tools, food, or clothing, the Negro needed some form of government aid. A vote on equal rights was a sanctimonious fraud without economic security.

But northern industry communicated to legislators such vistas of Midwest plains teeming with harvest and herds of cattle, such visions of virgin mines in the Southwest and golden splendors in the Rockies and on the Pacific coast, all waiting for initiative, money, and settlers, that the idea of voting any permanence to a social agency dedicated to doling out dollar and cents to the idle became a matter of the utmost impatience. If the Bureau developed solvent, accredited Republican voters who would recognize business as their chief friend, guide, and adviser, then it might serve a practical purpose. But a Bureau which talked endlessly of taking public or confiscated lands and passing them out in small parcels to indigent blacks induced profound uneasiness in the hearts of men who regarded any confiscation of land—unless for railroads and projects of sweeping development—as overt hostility to unlimited enterprise.

Stevens, in the House, led the fight for the Freedmen's Bureau. He was "The master spirit of the Congress," with an "astonishing control over the unwilling minds of others," a contemporary wrote at the time. This power was due to "A will of inherent and uncommon might, a perfect indifference to praise or blame, an invincible and incorruptible moral sense."

His desk was piled with reports and questions. Who, if

not the Freedmen's agent, was going to stand with the Negroes on a lonely road? Who was going to intervene when a contract was not honored? Who was going to guarantee a Negro's right to go to school?

Stevens' speeches usually began with a "grandfatherly grumbling . . . sometimes incoherent, always with a tone of muffled goodwill." He gave the impression of "hunting mislaid notes or a dropped handkerchief . . . Then rising erect, he lifts his long right arm with a wide sweep and with a sudden straight thrust of his long yellow finger, he sends forth in a thundering tone, the iron bolt of his argument." Food, clothes, medical supplies, transportation for the poor white and Negro—who else had authority to provide them but the Freedmen's Bureau? The confiscated acres—which were by no means enough—must be supplemented by public land in Flordia, Mississippi, Alabama, Louisiana, Arkansas. The acres must then be broken in forty-acre parcels and rented at ten cents an acre to those who applied, the Freedmen's Bureau acting as government broker.

Stevens said, "We have turned loose four million slaves without a hut to shelter them or a cent in their pockets. The infernal laws of slavery have prevented them from acquiring an education, understanding the commonest laws of contract, or of managing the ordinary business life. This Congress is bound to provide for them until they can take care of themselves. If we do not furnish them with homesteads and hedge them about with protective laws; if we leave them to the legislation of their late masters, we had better have left them in bondage."

Congress asked the President to give it a specific report on southern conditions. He offered Grant's. Grant had made a five-day journey and talked exclusively to the old-fashioned men. His report was muffled and cautious. Sumner, in the Senate, made a fierce, brilliant speech saying the President wished to "whitewash" the conditions of terror. He demanded that Schurz's report be given priority, and then he piled high on the heads of reluctant senators his own information which had come to him from Union officers, teachers, travelers.

"All expect the Negro to be killed in one way or another by emancipation. The policy of those who will eventually became the leaders here at the South is, for the present: to accept the best they can get, to acquiesce in anything and everything, but to strain every nerve to regain the political power and ascendancy they held . . . If the Northern people are content to be ruled over by the Southerners, they will continue in the Union. If not, the first chance they get they will rise again.

"In parts where there are no Union soldiers I saw colored women treated in the most outrageous manner. They have no rights that are respected. They are killed and their bodies are thrown into ponds or mud holes. They are mutilated by having ears and noses cut off."

For weeks Schurz had gone into hospitals and taken testimony from Negroes who had been half-killed and rescued by some Union soldier or Freedman's agent. "The emancipation of the slaves is submitted to only in so far as chattel slavery in the old forms could not be kept up . . . Wherever I go—the street, the shop, the house, the hotel, or the steamboat—I hear the people talk in such a way as to indicate that they are yet unable to conceive of the Negro as possessing any rights at all. Men who are honorable in their dealings with their white neighbors will cheat a Negro without feeling a single twinge of their honor. To kill a Negro they do not deem murder; to debauch a Negro woman, they do not think fornication; to take the property away from a Negro they do not consider robbery. The people boast that when they get the freedmen's affairs in their own hands, to use their expression, 'the niggers will catch hell.' "

Many Negroes had come to him in the dark of the night to say they had agreed to bad work contracts only because they had been beaten half to death and no Freedmen agent was near enough to intervene. Some Negroes were shot down who came to claim their wives and children.

General W. E. Strong, of the Freedmen's Bureau, reported to the Committee of Fifteen that the condition of the freedmen was worse in Texas than in any other southern state. A hundred and twenty-five thousand slaves had been shipped there during the war for safekeeping, and in their efforts to return to their old homes, "They are frequently beaten unmercifully, shot down like wild beasts, followed with hounds, and maltreated in every possible way. Two thirds of the freedmen in the section which I travelled over have never received one cent of wages since they were declared free" (though an immense crop of cotton, corn and sugar had been harvested).

In the Senate and the House the true reason for the hatred of the Bureau was laid on the line: the white planters wanted no interference with their laborers. The Bureau, in a report to Congress, had said that the Black Codes "actually served to secure to the former slaveholding class the unpaid labor which they had been accustomed to enjoy before the war." The presence of the Bureau was a constant reminder that times had changed.

Early in February 1866 a bill to extend the Bureau's life for another year was passed. Again there was no appropriation, only a recommendation of faith. The bill went to Johnson.

The veto was written by Seward. The bill was unconstitutional, the veto said. It created dependence. "It was never intended that freedmen should be fed, clothed, educated and sheltered by the United States. The idea upon which slaves were assisted to freedom was that they become a self-sustaining population . . ." Their wages were protected by the laws of supply and demand. Let him apply to the laws of his own state if he felt in any danger.

Congress was deeply shaken. The Republicans were afraid to challenge Johnson too vigorously, for the Democrats loomed over them like a storm cloud. "The leading commercial men, who had become weary of war, contemplated with positive dread the reopening of a controversy," James G. Blaine, Speaker of the House, wrote in his *Twenty Years in Congress*. "The bankers of the great cities . . . believed harmonious cooperation was needed to reinstate confidence among the people. Against obstacles so menacing, against resistance so ominous, it seemed an act of boundless temerity to challenge the President."

The veto stood.

Alabama, South Carolina, Florida, Virginia, and Louisiana passed additional Black Codes. Even Seward, it was said, was disappointed and greatly embarrassed.

The Nation asked a practical question: What would be the effect on Congress if fifty-eight new representatives and twenty-two senators arrived in Congress as spokesmen and sponsors of these Black Codes and were finally seated?

On Washington's Birthday, Johnson stood in front of the White House and made a strange wild speech, as his supporters shouted and the flames of torches leaped. He named his friends and his enemies. His friends were the southern and northern Democrats. His enemies were "Thaddeus Stevens of Pennsylvania . . . Charles Sumner of Massachusetts . . . Wendell Phillips of Massachusetts. Do they want more blood? I am not afraid of assassins!"

Congress, more alarmed than it had ever been in its history, thrust the Civil Rights Bill through the two houses. Johnson vetoed it. He said Chinese, Indians, gypsies would become citizens if the Negro had his rights, that the bill was, in fact, "a discrimination against the white race."

Even the conservative Republicans voted to override the veto.

A new Freedmen's Bureau Bill was hastily offered, passed, and voted. Congress scarcely moved a muscle. Without debate the bill passed over the veto. "Nearly the whole Senate and auditory were carried off their feet and joined in a tumultuous outburst of cheering such as never heard in these halls before," a reporter sent word to his paper.

This last veto was one of Johnson's most foolish acts. "No-body can yet see the end," Sumner wrote. "Congress will not yield. The President is angry and brutal. Seward is the marplot. In the cabinet, on the question of the last veto, there were four against it to three for it." The time for a final test had come. In the House Stevens' power had grown like a whirlwind. His moral position was the basis of his power.

He had a profound sense of identification with the Negroes. He believed that the dignity of the white man in the South must not depend on the degradation of the Negro.

A Fourteenth Amendment had become imperative. It was needed to make "inoperative and void" any laws "whereby distinction is made in civil or political rights or privileges on account of race, creed or color."

The Fourteenth Amendment, as it came out of committee, did not satisfy him and it did not satisfy Sumner (who in January had opposed the admission of the new states of Colorado and Nebraska because they did not give a vote to the Negro). The amendment gave the Negro the name of citizen but his right to vote was left ambiguous.

On July 28, 1866, the day Congress adjourned, Stevens made his last great plea for Negro citizenship. He was seventy-three years old. His health was almost gone. "It is easy," he said, when he rose that day in the House, "to protect the interests of the rich and powerful, but it is a great labor to guard the rights of the poor and downtrodden . . . I believe we must all account hereafter for deeds done in the body, and that political deeds will be among those accounts. I desire to take to that bar of the final settlement the record that I shall this day make on the great question of human rights."

Two days later New Orleans was bathed in riot.

57

It was a riot in some ways unprecedented for brutality. The governor was a Louisianan named James M. Wells, a large planter though he had opposed secession. He wanted the planters in power again and yet he wanted all the benefits of the Union. General Philip Sheridan, commanding the military district of Louisiana and Texas, had told Secretary of War Stanton that Wells was both a political trickster and a dishonest man.

Louisiana Negroes had been educated in rights and privileges since Union forces had taken New Orleans. Not only Negroes of education but freed slaves had developed great political acumen in the long incubation. It was plain to practical politicians like Wells that some accommodation would have to be made.

However, the planters had determined that Louisiana should also have a constitutional convention. They were determined if possible to overthrow the constitution of 1864, and the legislature passed a bill by a two-thirds majority requiring that the slave constitution of 1861 be restored.

Governor Wells was on the horns of a terrible dilemma. If this action was carried he foresaw the wrath of Congress and his own political death. He decided to reconvene the constitutional convention of 1864, which would automatically require some recognition of Negro suffrage.

The excitement was enormous. Wells became frightened and disappeared. He induced a member of that 1864 convention to issue the call for a meeting on July 30, 1866, instead of himself.

On July 30 New Orleans looked like a city under siege. The mayor of New Orleans, who was also head of the secret society called The Southern Cross, had armed the police and a mob which converged on the hall where the convention was meeting. About one hundred and fifty people, mostly Negroes, were present in the hall. The Reverend Mr. Horton, one of the delegates, waved a white handkerchief and shouted to the police, "I beseech you to stop firing; we are noncombatants. If you want to arrest us, do that!" The police replied, it was claimed, "We don't want any prisoners. You've all got to die."

Between thirty-eight and forty-eight were killed and one hundred and forty-eight wounded. General Sheridan said, "It was no riot. It was an absolute massacre by the police . . . a murder which the mayor and police perpetrated without the shadow of necessity . . . At least nine-tenths of the casualties were perpetrated by the police and citizens by stabbing and smashing in the heads of many who had already been wounded or killed by policemen."

All the individual acts of terror in the South seemed drawn together by this riot, and they gave a ghastly answer to an inadequate Fourteenth Amendment. The political alignments that had lingered after the death of Lincoln came to an end that July day. Three members of Johnson's Cabinet, Postmaster General William Dennison, Secretary of the Interior James Harlan, and Attorney General James Speed, resigned.

In August the disintegration was carried a step further when a "Johnson" convention was called in Philadelphia. This was a year of northern state and congressional elections, and Johnson planned to fill the next Congress with his friends if humanly possible.

Some "Johnsonized" Republicans attended the convention but most of the delegates were either Southerners or that breed of prosouthern Northerner known as "Copperhead." Every southern state was represented, and drama reached a climax when Confederate and Union officers marched in two by two, arms linked.

The Republicans called a "loyal" convention, also in Philadelphia. They too invited delegates from the South— if they brought petitions for Negro suffrage. During that hot midsummer of 1866, the country lay weltering in an incoherence of aborted plans, half-born policies, fear, dismay, and state elections. Johnson, like a man beset, started "swinging around the circle" of the North. He demanded that Grant accompany him.

Grant had remained an unblemished hero. Grant was very reluctant. Although he was far from being a Radical Republican, and although his report on the South had been an equivocal document, he knew, as General of the Army (he was the first to hold this rank since Washington) much more than he had written down. He had supported the Freedmen's Bureau and he had even recommended that every officer on duty in the South "should be regarded as an agent of the Bureau. This would create responsibility and give uniformity of action throughout the South." He still held to the belief that five generations of uncontested rule could not be overcome in months—he counseled patience—but he had also a realistic compassion for the Negro.

Grant was not happy on this tour.

"Hang Thad Stevens!" was the cry Johnson sent up from public squares and public halls. "Who was responsible for the New Orleans riot? Thad Stevens! Hang him!" Grant bore with this, chewing his cigar and saying nothing. When a heckler in St. Louis shouted, "Hang Jeff Davis!" Johnson shouted back, "Hang Thad Stevens and Wendell Phillips!"

Johnson seldom spoke directly about the Negro, but he said again and again that he did not want the Southerners back in the Union if they came "a degraded and debased people. I want them to come back with all their manhood."

The tour became a nightmare. Johnson, like a man possessed—or drunk, as the northern newspapers claimed—shook his fist at the towns draped in black to greet him, at the bands which played the death march, at the curt refusal of governors to meet him.

He returned to Washington a discomfited and disgraced man. He had succeeded in making Congress overwhelmingly Republican, overwhelmingly hostile, and had given northern industry occasion for profound second thoughts.

The substance of the second thoughts ran like this: The states reconstructed by Johnson are filled with killings. Prosperity depends on peace. Peace depends on men who can act as independent citizens, working, trading, voting. Let us increase prosperity by making more buyers and voters, even if they are all Negro.

If the Constitution must be amended, let us do so.

If our proposal puts us in advance of our times, let time catch up with us.

Hunger was taking a frightful toll in the South. The Freedmen's Bureau reported starvation in some counties. In the mountains of northern Alabama white men died of hunger, and in March 1867, famine reached the coast. Governor Orr of South Carolina said that more than 100,000 had not tasted meat in a month and thousands had no bread. General Howard made all the facilities of the Freedmen's Bureau available to whites as well as Negroes. To protests he replied, "The rebellion is over, people are starving."

The effect on the poor whites was revolutionary. When they found that the rations which kept them alive came not from their old lords, the planters, but from the friends of free elections, free schools and free lands, they blinked and gave it a thought. For three generations these men had been stunted. Their free hands had been chained by enforced competition with slavery and their minds drugged by the narcotic of their white skins. This had proved no substitute for food.

They leaned on the fences and talked to the Negroes next door.

The speed with which the Fourteenth Amendment came before the state legislatures showed the changing temper of the times. In half the northern states it was ratified before the autumn. In all the southern states it was rejected.

In January the second session of the 39th Congress

61

came together in anger. Dismay was verging on fright. The coalition was splitting dangerously. Johnson tried to make a virtue of riots and recalcitrance; disorders were merely an indication of the unrest of a land recovering from war. Slavery had been legally abolished, he pointed out, in every state but Mississippi, where the Thirteenth Amendment had not been ratified. The Negro was "an object of deep concern to those who know him best"—which had a heavy traditional meaning but could also be translated in another sense: there were many men in the South who knew that there would be no salvation for man or beast if the Negro were not allowed his manhood.

Congress turned a stony face to its President. The Fourteenth Amendment was a singularly mild document; Johnson had intervened in its behalf by speeches and letters to southern governors; yet it had been totally refused.

To Sumner this was a matter of bad morals. "Anything for human rights is constitutional." To Stevens morality must be supported by the most cogent and effective politics. He was prepared to fight Johnson on his own ground —Johnson who had during the summer replaced 1,283 Republican postmasters with Democrats; Johnson, the Republican President, who promised to "kick" Republicans out of other branches of government "just as fast as I can."

Stevens was also shocked by the support the Supreme Court was giving to Johnson. Stevens had never been an iconolator as far as the Constitution was concerned. To him it was a document which must be susceptible to human needs, and he saw profound danger in the Court's deepening orthodoxy toward states' rights.

Ruling in the case of a Confederate sympathizer who had been sentenced to death by a military commission, the Court decided by a 5 to 4 decision that neither Congress nor the President possessed the power to institute such military commission except in the actual theater of war where the civil courts were not open.

The decision—an undoubted safeguard in ordinary times—would not have alarmed the Republicans if Johnson had not immediately shown what he intended to do with the decision: render the Union army powerless to function as a police force.

Without the troops, polling places and schools could not survive, not to mention the Republican newspapers established here and there to balance the angry outpourings of the old Democratic sheets.

The troops were spread very thinly over the South. Between January and May of 1866, all Negro troops in Mississippi—8,784 soldiers and 338 officers (mostly noncommissioned)—had been mustered out. White replacements were often apathetic and inclined to accept the viewpoint of the white Southerner who offered hospitality.

And Johnson's constant invoking of civilian authority merely drew attention (as several of his opponents pointed out) to such disinterested actions by civilian authority as the New Orleans riot which had been organized and led by the mayor and the police.

But with the Court decision Johnson ordered all pending trials of civilians by the military dismissed. Men facing trial for the murder of Negroes or Union soldiers were released from prison, and those who had already been sentenced became busy with appeals.

Even to conservative northern men, the Supreme Court decision cast as deep and troubling a shadow as the Dred Scott decision had ten years before.

It was said and believed that the Court would declare the Thirteenth and Fourteenth Amendments unconstitutional.

CHARGES of political opportunism did not disturb the Republicans. Loosely joined, they still represented one hundred and forty-three members in the House and forty-two in the Senate. Of course they wanted the vote of the Negro; they deserved it, they were the party of Lincoln.

Democratic ideology in Congress was just as clear-cut. Their membership stood at forty-nine in the House and eleven in the Senate. The party of the extreme conservative South, it needed and wanted the vote of the conservative South. If this raised an old fear—and congressmen with sensitive memories invoked the time when the South had dominated Congress—the northern Democrats believed that northern economics would allow *them* to control the balance.

Such firm and candid party attitudes brought enormous comfort.

Alabama Negroes, meeting in Mobile, sent a message to the Committee of Fifteen. "Several of their churches have been already burned to the ground . . . the means of education are secured to them only by the strong arm of the United States government . . . A respectful appeal to the late State convention [for franchise] was scornfully laid upon the table, some of the members even refusing to hear its reading. Many of their people daily suffer almost every form of outrage and violence. They are knocked down and beaten without cause; they are arrested and imprisoned upon false accusations; their money is extorted for their release or they are condemned to imprisonment at forced labor. Many of their people are being compelled to serve their former owners without pay and to call them 'master.' They express a hope that Congress may be led to give them an opportunity to verify these statements by suitable testimony and also . . . grant them the protection they need."

Stevens rose to speak for this. His face was gray, his voice hardly audible. He had only a few more months of life. His eyes, set far behind his overjutting brows, were like the caves of some awful god, his old black wig sat grotesquely askew. But this remnant of a human being had such inner fire and power that no one was deceived by his appearance.

He became a holy terror.

He faced Congress and the country with a sheaf of bills designed to break the power of Johnson, cancel the decision of the Supreme Court, and establish, for a time at least, a new concept of government by the governed. Congress was to have supreme authority. The American constitution with its checks and balances might call this tyranny, but in fact his proposals were close to the British Parliamentary system.

His evidence was in his hand. It was not legalistic; it was human. Man was not made for the law; the law was made for man. "A perfect Republic" was his vision.

He spread his affidavits before his colleagues . . . hundreds of Negroes convicted of petty crimes had been sold into slavery. In Florida, a Negro guilty of assault and battery was given to a master for twenty years. In Memphis, the chief of police imprisoned Negroes charged with no crime or misdemeanor and then hired them out to any planter who applied for them. Freedmen's agents were, day by day, rescuing Negro children "apprenticed" under the Black Codes into involuntary servitude.

From Mississippi the commanding general reported that only one white man had been convicted, in the past twelve months, for the killing of a Negro. His sentence was one year in jail. Five hundred indictments for murder in Texas had been returned against white men and not one conviction obtained.

In South Carolina stood an open offer: to kill for a fixed sum any freedmen who refused to sign a work contract.

Terror had a dreary repetition: a Negro castrated and then murdered . . . Another shot off his mule "because the ruffian thought it more trouble to ask him to get off than to shoot him."

"Careful investigation has proven that the worst outrages [are] generally committed by small bands of lawless men, organized under various names, whose principal objects [are] robbery and plunder and to prevent what was denominated 'negro domination.' "

Stevens now had the Republican contingent of the 39th Congress behind him almost to a man, a phenomenon that can perhaps be explained only by the fact that the issues were so well defined—and aided, one must add, by his remarkable skill, his power of invective, and the enlightenment that had fallen on northern business. Fourteen million buyers and voters . . . Old Abolition sentiment stirred again, putting the Negro at the heart of the matter.

The vote for Negro suffrage in the District was brought up as a practice for the skirmish. The bill was passed. Johnson vetoed it. He argued that it was an anachronism since Negroes were denied the right to vote in many northern states.

When the bill returned to Congress, the galleries of the House and all the ways leading to the Capitol were filled with crowds of whites and Negroes, very quiet, very anxious. The roll call was taken and a great shout went in waves from the galleries along the corridors out into the January day as the veto was overridden.

The vote was almost like a token designed to hold the line while the more complicated skirmishing went on. Johnson's hands must now be tied.

"It is possible that the President may be impeached," Sumner said. "If we go forward and supersede the sham governments set up in the rebel states, we encounter the appointing power of the President who would put in office men who sympathize with him," thus controlling government in a time of crisis.

Johnson was dismissing and confirming like a king. He was using every prerogative in his power. The Senate pressed toward one danger that must be forestalled. They must prevent the dismissal by the President of officeholders appointed by the Senate. A Tenure of Office Bill was drafted. The House insisted the bill must cover Cabinet members as well, for Edwin Stanton, the Secretary of War, was already in danger.

In the House the primary step toward Congressional Reconstruction was taken. From the Committee of Fifteen came the declaration that life and property would not be safe in the southern states until loyalty to constitutional amendments was assured. A bill was offered dividing the South into five military divisions. The commanding generals were made responsible for calling new constitutional conventions which would take universal suffrage as their first requirement.

The bill was debated day after day—at a remarkable high level of argument and of profound concern for the future. Caucus after caucus wrestled with its substance, and votes were often by slippery margins. The Republicans, conservative and Radical, held together. By February 2o, 1867, the bill had passed both Houses and been sent to Johnson.

Congress was to adjourn on March 4, and Johnson waited the full time allowed by law before he vetoed both bills.

The Republicans in the House promptly moved that the rules be suspended. Over the fervent protests of the Democrats, the bill was passed and sent to the Senate in the few hours left.

When the 39th Congress adjourned, the 40th immediately declared itself in session, thus making impossible the interregnum for which Johnson had been waiting. Sumner rose promptly to offer a new sheaf of bills—homes and schools for freedmen, a permanent policy of federal aid to education. But the Senate was too dizzy with its own exploration of power. These bills did not come to a vote. Sumner tried to get "white" struck out of naturalization bills. He failed. He tried to amend the Reconstruction Acts to provide free schools for all. A tie defeated him.

To his colleagues Sumner was exasperating and omniscient. He missed nothing that wore the look of slavery. A system of peonage in New Mexico brought out, almost overnight, his bill to abolish and forever prohibit it.

Stevens immediately offered a series of resolutions which would support the old wartime Confiscation Act of 1862. He spoke with brilliance and pungency of guilt and innocence, of land and the dispossessed, of forty acres and a mule. Everywhere the Negro was still refusing to surrender his land: in Richmond, Union troops had been obliged to put down an uprising when several hundred Negroes refused to pay rent on land they had been cultivating.

"More than $2,000,000,000 of property belonging to the United States, confiscated not as rebel but as enemy property, has been given back to enrich traitors." The small landowners should be secure in their land, but the great lords of the land, the "leading rebels" should lose their property in forty-acre tracts. The rest should be sold to pay the debts of the war. Thus the former slaves would be cared for, the leaders of the rebellion would pay for the war, and the national debt would be taken from about the necks of the people, "yet nine-tenths of the southern people would remain untouched."

He saw the strength of the new South that would emerge with Congressional Reconstruction as lying with

68

the landowning small farmers. But the planters saw this as well.

"Without confiscation," an Alabama editor wrote, "the result of Negro suffrage will slip through their fingers." This simple realism was shared by the Democrats, and Stevens was defeated.

Congress immediately passed a supplementary Reconstruction Bill, putting the machinery of election into the hands of the generals commanding the five military districts.

The old-fashioned South protested vehemently against this "terrible measure." The voices became quite incoherent about the peace prevailing in the land, the general order and happiness. The southern press, unfettered in any way, made stern strictures against federal encroachment on the right of states to determine their voters. And "living apes" or other quadrupeds were unfailingly referred to in the general context of the debate.

In April of this year, 1867, the Ku Klux Klan was formed in Nashville. In the Maxwell House, a large new hotel, men representing all the groups of night riders and "regulators" from Alabama to Virginia met under the leadership of General Nathan Bedford Forrest, the former slave trader who had commanded the massacre at Fort Pillow. They agreed upon the political uses of economic intimidation and simple terror.

Johnson as Commander in Chief had an unassailable position. Through a careful selection of the generals chosen to implement the new Reconstruction legislation, he could control the results. He ordered the removal of the two generals who would be most sympathetic to the enforcement of the Reconstruction Acts in their district: Philip Sheridan and Daniel Sickles.

Sheridan's district included Texas and Louisiana; Sickles', the Carolinas. Sheridan was replaced by Major General Winfield Scott Hancock, a man thoroughly loyal to

Johnson. Sickles was replaced by a subservient Brigadier General Edward R. S. Canby.

Sheridan's removal caused both jubilation and dismay in the South. The Union League held a huge protest meeting near New Orleans and asked that Johnson be deposed.

Grant was aghast, especially at the dismissal of Sheridan, his close friend. As General of the Army he demanded that Johnson rescind the order. Johnson replied by asserting his prerogative. Grant replied by overruling General Hancock as often as his sense of probity allowed.

Congress replied, too. The Act of July 19, 1867, required that "all so-called governments of the South should be subject to the orders of the District Commanders and the General of the Army and not the President. The boards of registration, set up by the commanders, would be sole judges of a man's fitness."

Before the bill passed the House, the power of appointing the five generals was taken from the President and put into the hands of Grant, with the additional provision that Grant was not to be removed during Johnson's term of office.

It was a dangerous precedent, but the House saw these as dangerous times. Grant himself asked that such a challenge to civilian control of the army not be made; the President was his Commander in Chief. The clause was rephrased. The appointments of the generals were to be made by the President and Stanton, the Secretary of War, with the advice and consent of General Grant, to whom the generals would be responsible.

Johnson vetoed it.

Both houses repassed it by a tremendous majority.

Talk of impeachment began again.

The tragedy was that, constitutionally speaking, Johnson was often right. What Congress was protesting was his adamant refusal to use congressional means to arrive at a *modus vivendi* with the future. Lincoln, with his sense of political reality and flexibility, would probably have found it. Johnson's temperament was a national calamity. He had warned the South over and over in speeches and letters to come to some terms, but he had done it in ways which merely deepened the impasse.

The Reconstruction Bill of February 20 said in effect that there were no trustworthy governments in Virginia, North and South Carolina, Georgia, Alabama, Mississippi, Louisiana, Florida, Texas, and Arkansas. Until governments representing all the citizens were voted into office, the five generals in command would be solely responsible for the life, liberty, and personal rights of all citizens— even to the extent of legal punishments and court decisions if a death sentence were involved.

This military rule would be immediately rescinded when a state "formed a constitution and government in conformity with the Constitution of the United States in all respects, framed by a convention of delegates elected by male citizens over 21 years of age of whatever race or color or previous condition of servitude . . . except such as might be disfranchised for rebellion or felony . . . this convention ratifying the Fourteenth Amendment."

Johnson, in some desperation, looked to the fall elections of 1867 as his salvation, yet in the interval he made several moves which snared him more deeply.

In September he extended a full pardon to Confederates (his previous amnesties had "left about one hundred thousand citizens outside the amnesty," said the *New York Tribune*; "this one leaves out one or two thousand") and urged them to test themselves without delay in the courts. They did. They flew to the courts. The governor of Mississippi tried to get an enjoinment to prevent the Reconstruction laws from being executed.

The Supreme Court decided that interference would not be proper.

Georgia attempted to enjoin the Secretary of War. The court held it was without jurisdiction.

All through the South this fall, congressional Reconstruction was beginning to sound like a dam breaking. Congress had ordered September registration of all voters, Negro and white, to determine whether new constitutional conventions should meet.

Southern Democrats were divided on tactics. Should every white man register and so control the new constitutional conventions? Or should the whites register and vote against the constitutional conventions? Or should they stay away from the pools and so invalidate registration?

The new generals whom Johson had appointed were hurriedly building support for the white conservatives by revoking many of the rulings of their liberal predecessors. Hancock, especially, made no effort to curb the Klan, and everywhere the registration was opened to the swift action of the "regulators" and the dismaying fact that the army wavered and almost broke.

In Mississippi the work was almost Sisyphean. In the raw desolate black counties the plantations ruled absolutely. Even the look in the eyes of the Negroes was different. Into this section freedmen's agents were reluctant to come; here Negro soldiers had little chance to stay alive. In these isolated kingdoms of southern Mississippi, slave uprisings had hardly ever taken place in the past, so harsh and binding was the control.

A few teachers had ventured here but did not survive long. "Four young men in Adams County conspired to murder the teacher of a Negro school . . . They maltreated him somewhat barbarously."

Under such circumstances Union Leagues were difficult to keep alive, but wherever they could gain a foothold they explained to the Negroes why it was important to resist the intimidation, and register, how to do it, the rights and duties of voting. They were supported in this by the new commanding general, Edward Ord, who cancelled the Black Codes by military order, thus breaking an ice-jam.

State machinery for registration had to be completely rebuilt. The Humphreys government refused to supply one pen or one bottle of ink. General Ord commanded that Negroes who could read and write in any fashion be included among the registrars.

He also appointed Isaiah T. Montgomery as a justice of the peace. Montgomery was a prosperous farmer. Before the war he had been business manager of one of the largest estates in the South, the plantation of Jefferson Davis. Montgomery had been Davis' slave. He was now the first Mississippi Negro to hold public office.

All these actions of Ord brought bitter cries from the old-fashioned Mississippians who called on "all lovers of peace throughout the country [to] condemn [the] order as injurious if not insulting to that race which God has created superior to the black man."

During the weeks of preparation for elections the tension grew. The cotton crop of 1867 had been a failure. There were widespread thefts of horses and crops. Planters were charged with driving their field hands off the estates when the time came for paying back wages. Fiery crosses and hooded riders were almost as familiar as the birds in the trees.

In the northern counties the Leagues had taken root and organized the Negroes to a great extent. On the day of registration the black voters came in by the thousands, together, like regiments, often carrying arms. The editor of the *Gazette,* in Raymond, said, "Our usually quiet village was enlivened on Monday by the presence from adjacent plantations of from 300 to 500 of the newly manufactured American citizens of African descent . . . We must give our newly made voters the benefit of the remark that they conducted themselves throughout the day with decorum and propriety, showing good breeding and a proper respect for 'the situation.' As a consequence upon their good behavior, the largest liberty was allowed them by the whites, and we are glad to perceive that they seemed to appreciate the kindness shown them."

They used their "largest liberty" to sweep in with them as voters the white men whose lack of property qualifications had never before allowed them to enter a polling place.

Some of the Negroes were disappointed with the results. They thought they had come to receive land.

For some time the white people of Mississippi had been firmly convinced that the Negro was dying out. The census of 1866 had appeared to confirm it. They were therefore deeply shocked by the results of the registration. The number of whites who had registered was 46,636 and the registered Negroes numbered 60,167.

Many whites determined, at that instant, to boycott the convention, which could not be called unless the required number of voters demanded it. Those 60,000 new Negro voters would be powerless as long as Mississippi remained out of the Union. Mississippi would remain out of the Union as long as the Thirteenth Amendment was not ratified. What would be the state's future with such an albatross around its neck? The status of an occupied province acquired great charm when seen in this way. "Shall Mississippi ratify the Thirteenth Amendment?" The *Vicksburg Herald* cried in November. "No! Ten thousand times No!"

A campaign of lively intimidation followed. Night riders pursued a steady course in the dark, and by day threatened to discharge all plantation workers who registered their names or put down their marks. The Union League answered the intimidation by counter activity. They paraded with guns. At rallies they reassured the Negroes, mocking the efforts to form a "white man's party," and called on white laborers to work with the Negroes in forming Republican organizations.

When the vote was counted, 76,016 Mississippians

wanted the convention, and had elected delegates and 6,277 did not. A Vicksburg newspaper offered a reward for the names of those "interesting sneaks," the eight white Vicksburgians who had cast their votes for the convention.

In Alabama a meeting called by Negroes for Negroes made a public statement setting forth their desires and the responsibility they would assume after registration had established their rights.

They asked their "fellow citizens" to recognize that they had the "same rights, privileges, and immunities as are enjoyed by white men. We ask for nothing more and will be content with nothing less . . . As long as a park or street is a public park or street the entire public has the right to use it. So long as a car or a steamboat is a public conveyance, it must carry all who come to it and serve all alike. The law no longer knows white or black but simply men, and consequently we are entitled to . . . hold office, sit on juries, and do everything else which in the past we were prevented from doing solely on the ground of our color . . . One half of the voters in Alabama are now black men, and in a few months there is to be an entire reorganization of the state government. The question which every man, now illegally discriminating against us, has to decide is whether it is politic to insist upon gratifying prejudice during a few dull months, with a certainty of incurring the lasting displeasure of one half of the voting population. We can stand it if they can.

"There are some good people who are always preaching patience. They would have us wait a few months, years or generations until the whites voluntarily give us our rights, but we do not intend to wait one day longer than we are absolutely compelled to.

"Look at our demands and then look at theirs. We ask of them simply that they surrender unreasonable and unreasoning prejudice: that they consent to allow others to

75

prosper and be happy. But they would have us pay for what we do not get; tramp through the broiling sun or pelting rain, or stand upon a platform while empty seats mockingly invite us to rest our wearied limbs. Our sick must suffer or submit to indignity. We must put up with inconvenience of every kind, and the virtuous aspirations of our children must be continually checked by the knowledge that no matter how upright their conduct, they will be looked on as less worthy of respect than the lowest wretch on earth who wears a white skin.

"The men who make such requests must think us devoid of spirit and of brains, but they will find themselves mistaken. Solemnly and distinctly we say to you again, men of Alabama, that we will not submit voluntarily to such infamous discrimination, and if you will insist upon trampling on the rights and outraging the feelings of those who are so soon to pass judgment upon you, then on your own heads will rest the responsibility for the effects of your course.

"Another fact should be borne in mind. While a few conservatives are making guarded promises to us, the masses of that party are cursing us and doing all they can to 'make the d-d niggers stay in their place.' If we were, therefore, to join that party, it would be simply as servants and not as equals. Some leaders who needed our votes might treat us decently but the great majority would expect us to stay at home until election day and then vote as our employer dictated. This we respectfully decline doing.

"The press of Mobile and other parts of the state contain numerous threats that those colored people who do not vote as their employers command will be discharged; that the property-holders will combine, import white laborers and discharge their colored hands. Numerous instances have come to our knowledge of persons who have already been discharged because they attended Republican meetings, and great numbers have been threatened.

76

". . . The most effectual method of preserving our unity will be for us to always act together—never to hold separate political meetings or caucuses. It may take some time for us to get to pulling together well, but perseverance and honest endeavor will overcome all obstacles. In nominations for office we expect that there will be no discriminations on account of color, but that the most capable and honest men will always be put in nomination. We understand full well that our people are too deficient in education to be generally qualified to fill the higher offices, but when qualified men are found they must not be rejected for being black.

"This lack of education which is the consequence of our long servitude and which so diminishes our powers for good, should not be allowed to characterize our children when they come upon the stage of action, and we therefore earnestly call upon the Republican party to demand the establishment of a thorough system of common schools throughout the state . . . With education secured to all, with the old and helpless properly cared for, with justice everywhere impartially administered, Alabama will commence a career of which she will have just cause to be proud."

About 1,363,000 now qualified as voters in ten Confederate states. Of these, 700,000 were Negroes. The whites who registered were obliged to take an "ironclad oath" of loyalty to the American constitution. Even if one includes "carpetbaggers" (those Northerners who had come to live in the South), and army men, the number of white Southerners who qualified and registered was impressive. Though some were conservatives who did it to insure a large registration and then, by failing to vote, defeat the new constitution, most were honest, poor and harassed men who wanted to get on with the future. These southern whites now had a power which they had never possessed under the rule of the land aristocracy. If these men had remained consistent to the end, great suffering could have been prevented.

One of the tragedies of Reconstruction was the failure of thousands of white Southerners to hold on, through thick and thin, to their innate conviction that a decent future could only be based on mutual respect. They shilly-shallyed; they tried to have it both ways. In the end their white neighbors felt only contempt and the Negroes only a deep apprehension.

The constitutional conventions would begin early in the new year 1868 to set up state governments.

Meanwhile, Johnson was going again among the torch-lights and the bands, uttering his hoarse cries against his enemies. The Negroes were "so ignorant of public affairs that their voting can consist in nothing more than carrying a ballot to the place where they are directed to deposit it . . . Of all the dangers which our nation had yet encountered, none are equal to those which must result from the success of the effort now making to Africanize the half of our country."

He was not a lone voice in a wilderness, for Ohio and Pennsylvania voted for the Democrats this fall and rejected Negro suffrage, and New York, New Jersey, and Maryland gave the Democrats large majorities. Money-panic was in the air and panic worked against the party in power.

Negroes had the vote in only eight northern states. In eight other states they had been rejected, and Southerners commented bitterly on the fact that they were being forced to accept a situation for which the North itself had little taste.

In December, when Congress reconvened, Johnson returned to his theme in the annual message. "Negroes have shown less capacity for government than any other race of people. No independent government of any form has ever been successful in their hands . . . whenever they have been left to their own devices they have shown a constant tendency to relapse into barbarism. In the southern states however, Congress has undertaken to confer upon them the privilege of the ballot . . ."

He dismissed his Secretary of War in a one-line letter.

Edwin Stanton was the only remaining member of the Cabinet with a thorough dislike of the Confederacy. He rejected the dismissal in one line of his own.

Johnson then suspended him and appointed Grant as interim secretary.

A dismayed Grant remonstrated, but he did it in private, so that his friends among the Radical Republicans (who were nursing Presidential dreams for him) were angry and disconcerted.

Johnson formally notified the Senate of his action in a direct effort to test the Tenure of Office Act.

Congress ordered Stanton to resume his duties, and Grant stepped down in momentary relief.

Grant had never had much liking for Johnson. He knew that he himself was being watched by powerful forces in the North. He had supported the Reconstruction acts as the only safety for the Negro and he had some political ambitions. He also had integrity and vast prestige. His support of the Reconstruction acts had drawn the attention of northern business, which at this precise moment was prepared to embrace any force, even Congress, which could hold in check the old agricultural oligarchy.

Passions were so high, the tension was so great, that rumors of a coup d'état by Johnson and the South—a new secession—ran like a brush fire. "I do not exaggerate," Carl Schurz wrote in his autobiography, "that an overwhelming majority of loyal Union men, north and south, saw in President Johnson a traitor bent upon turning over the national government to the rebels again, and ardently wished to see him stripped of power, not so much for what he had done but for what, as they thought, he was capable of doing and likely to do."

Johnson dismissed Stanton again, and the machinery of impeachment was wheeled into place.

☆ 6 ☆

1 8 6 8 W A S the most revolutionary year in American history. It was the beginning of a short period when certain fundamental principles of democracy were brought into the light and never quite lost sight of again.

It was not a period of "Negro rule." Only in states where Negroes outnumbered the whites—Mississippi and South Carolina—did they hold the decisive power. When they did, they used it "as citizens of the state."

In South Carolina the Negroes represented 60 percent of the people and 63 percent of the registered voters. In Mississippi the Negroes were 55 percent of the people and the majority of the registered electorate. (Mississippi did not give statistics by color.) In Louisiana the Negroes were 50 percent of the people, 65 percent of the voters.

Reconstruction in the South did not proceed in a single pattern. It proceeded according to the enlightenment or the exigencies of each individual state.

The best way to dispel the myths of Reconstruction is to know the facts.

On December 3, 1867, the first of the new constitutional conventions met. It took place in Richmond, Virginia. Twenty-five Negroes were delegates and eighty whites. The Virginia press referred to it as a convention of kangaroos. This was unkind, for many friends of the press, rabidly anti-Negro, were delegates.

When the preamble of a Bill of Rights was taken up, James Bland, a Negro, moved that the clause "that all men are by nature equally free and independent" yield to a better phrase: "all mankind, irrespective of race and color."

"Men," he said, "has been construed to mean white men only in Virginia, whereas 'mankind' takes in all the men, women and children on earth."

Free public education took up the greatest time of discussion. The Negroes insisted on mixed schools. The final report did not specify either mixed or separate schools, but education for all. The Negroes insisted on universal suffrage, and prevailed when every man over twenty-one was given the vote.

There were as many resolutions as delegates. One delegate moved that a man should not lose his job for his political opinions. Another moved that work should be decently paid for. "Six dollars a month will not pay a man and feed and clothe his wife and children," insisted Mr. Bayne, who called himself an ignorant field hand.

Taxes were imposed on incomes over $600. Counties were ordered reorganized to break the control of several landed families which had ruled the state.

Plans for submitting the constitution to the voters were brought to a sudden halt. General J. M. Schofield, the commanding general, disliked the whole proceeding so much that he refused to authorize money for the election.

Republicans appealed to Congress for a sepcial appropriation. The matter dragged on like a curious dream until July 1869, when President Grant finally ordered an election and the constitution was accepted. The new governor (a conservative named Walker who disliked Negroes), the frustrations imposed on the convention, the calculated delays, the triumph of the conservatives in the election— these were all considered "a Confederate victory."

The *Lynchburg Virginian* said, "The deluded Negroes have been taught a lesson which will bring them to their senses and we shall have no more trouble with them."

Under these circumstances, the Republicans in Congress tried to prevent the admission of Virginia, but Grant wanted it back in whatever condition, and Virginia was restored to the Union in February 1870.

Twenty-seven Negroes did serve in the subsequent legislature, however, and one distinguished Negro came to Washington from Louisa County as congressman. John Mercer Langston was born a slave, was educated at Oberlin College in Ohio, and was admitted to the bar. He recruited Negro soldiers for the Union army, became a member of the Board of Education in Oberlin, acted as general inspector of freedmen's schools for the Bureau, and suddenly found himself in the embarrassing position of arguing President Johnson out of the notion of appointing him to supersede General Howard as head of the Bureau. Langston was admitted to practice before the Supreme Court in 1867, but continued his peripatetic career as inspector of freedmen's schools which took him to every state in the South.

In 1869 he became Dean of the Law School of the shining new Howard University, in Washington, that splendid jewel of freedmen's education, chartered in 1867 with General Howard as its first President.

He was a highly cultivated man and he made an excellent congressman.

Georgia, on December 9, 1867, met in convention. Some weeks earlier 93,457 Negroes and 95,214 whites had registered. In 1860, 102,585 white voters had registered. The convention sat until the middle of March. There were 169 delegates, 37 of whom were Negroes and

9 white carpetbaggers. White Georgians were in control. Most of them were Democrats.

The *Savannah News* allowed that "the Negroes in the convention appeared well-dressed and well-behaved with few exceptions."

Suffrage, free schools, and full civil rights were the first concern.

Atlanta University was chartered this year for Negro students. (Augusta Institute, later to be called Morehouse College, was also chartered, and so was Talladega in Alabama.)

In January 1866, a few Georgia Negroes had formed the Georgia Educational Association because they knew how important it was for freedmen to be responsible for the establishing and support of schools. By 1867 an informal count showed 191 day schools and 45 night schools. Nearly a hundred of them were supported by the Freedmen's Bureau, who held title to 57 of the schoolhouses.

Georgia was the only southern state with a degree of industrial development. Several white Georgians had made modest fortunes in railways and factories, and these men were invariably antislavery. Several of them sat in this convention, sincerely and honorably supporting the Negro demands. These demands were presented by such men as Aaron Bradley, who seemed afraid of no one, and fought Republicans and Democrats impartially if he felt they were yielding to expediency. Racial discrimination on public vehicles, unlawful imprisonment of Negroes—or of anyone for that matter—were two issues he did not let rest. For three years he had struggled to protect the Negro holdings on the Sea Islands.

White men did not like him. The Negroes had unbounded confidence.

Tunis Campbell had come from Massachusetts as a Freedmen's Bureau agent. He too had fought the matter of land on the Sea Islands. There he had set up an armed community which yielded only when the odds against them had too many guns. He too was a great power among the Negroes. He threw all his efforts toward forcing the convention to abolish imprisonment for debt.

Henry McNeal Turner was, in time, one of the best known of the Negro politicians in the South. He had been born in South Carolina; Lincoln had made him an army chaplain. When the war ended, he joined the Freedmen's Bureau. From his travels as an agent he knew Georgia from corner to corner and he became a tireless speech-maker for the Republicans. The Methodists made him a bishop; he showed his Christian spirit by trying to get a pardon for Jefferson Davis. But he was heartily disliked by white men, and, he said later, "arrested and tried on the wildest and most groundless accusations ever distilled from the laboratory of hell."

The constitution—which in addition to the essentials of civil rights included relief from taxes and foreclosures—was adopted and Rufus Bullock became governor. Bullock was born in the North but he had moved to Georgia before the Civil War and had served in the Confederate army.

In 1869, when Georgia would not ratify the Fifteenth Amendement, a bill was passed in Congress refusing to admit the state back into the Union until the amendment had been accepted, and sending home the representatives. Once more Georgia came under military rule, and General Meade, commanding in the state, showed an iron hand. The legislature met under his stern frown in January 1870 and ratified both the Fourteenth and Fifteenth Amendments, recognized all the colored members who had been ousted, and showed general repentance by paying their salaries retroactively.

Georgia representatives were admitted to the 41st Congress, and among them was a new delegate, Jefferson Long, who spoke stubbornly and persistently against the

Klan outrages. He was a Negro born in Crawford County, self-educated, who had gone into business as a merchant tailor in Macon.

The Negroes once again began to show some control of legislation. Henry McNeal Turner alone introduced a series of bills to establish a state police, secure a penitentiary system that would protect prisoners from exploitation, give more support to the Georgia State Orphans' Home, and amend the constitution of Georgia so that women could vote. Only a few of his bills went through. Woman remained without the vote.

A report in 1875 made an interesting analysis of Georgia's citizens. "There are many colored mechanics and they receive full wages where they are skillful. Near Atlanta, they own small truck-farms and supply the market with vegetables. There are fewer black than white beggars in the cities; and a missionary clergyman surprised me by the remark that the blackberry crop, which was ripening, was a blessing to dozens of poor white families whom he knew who lived half the year in a condition of semi-starvation."

For one year, 1870, the Republicans had a majority in both houses. In 1871, white defections began. The scalawags, whose allegiance to the Republicans was very tentative, joined the Democrats; the planters once more gained control, and that was the end of Reconstruction in Georgia. Congress refused to struggle with the problem again.

On January 7, 1868, the Arkansas convention met at Little Rock. It had eight Negro delegates, including a postmaster, two farmers, and four ministers. Registration had been a slow business; white men had told the Negroes the registration was to enroll them for taxes. Freedmen's Bureau agents intervened and carefully instructed them in the purposes of schools, the vote, equal justice at county levels. The constitution was a good one in spite of a Klan which ran the state pretty much in its own way.

Two days later Mississippians met in Jackson. The jokers called it the "black and tan" convention. There were one hundred delegates. Sixteen were Negroes although thirty-two counties had Negro majorities. The eighty-four white delegates were of all classes and classifications and included twenty-odd Union soldiers and carpetbaggers who represented some of the Negro counties.

Mississippi can be studied with profit as one end of the spectrum, the darkest. In the days of slavery it had been the center of the commercialized cotton kingdom. The greatest dread of slaves was to be sold into Mississippi. The plantations had no veneer of civilized life, for the planters had their homes in northern cities, or in New Orleans or Charleston, and seldom interrupted the raw and brutal regimens of the overseers who ruled like kings, their sole duty the production of cotton whatever the cost to humanity.

Even the war had barely touched the great power of the plantations. Many of the Negroes had been brutalized, and most were confused by freedom. The planters regained control with little opposition. The only leadership came from the nine thousand Negro soldiers who in 1865 had been posted in the state. They had been mustered out within the past year, but many of them had remained in Mississippi and a few now sat in Jackson as delegates. Among the Negro delegates were two especially interesting men. Both bore the name of Lynch though they were not related. The Reverend James D. Lynch was the man who had helped to establish the schools in Savannah under General Sherman. Sent to Mississippi by both the Methodists and the Freedmen's Bureau, he had become a presiding elder of the church in Jackson as well as a Bureau agent. He was a sophisticated and highly competent man, and he was to become Mississippi's Secretary of State.

The other Lynch, John Roy, born a slave in Louisiana, had been brought to Natchez by his mother's purchaser, freed by the Union troops, and educated by the Freed-

86

men's Bureau. He was twenty-one years old and a photographer in Natchez. In time he would become Speaker of the Mississippi House of Representatives and later a congressman.

Before the convention settled to the business of discussing a constitution, three of the Negro delegates signed a petition asking that money be set aside from the public fund to help former slaves, sold years ago into Mississippi, find their way back to old homes and families. They also asked the governor of the state, Confederate General Benjamin Humphreys, to allow Negroes a share in the donations sent to him for the relief of the poor and disabled.

General Humphreys refused. He said the money was a private gift.

A white delegate rose and asked for a ruling, before the convention started, which would require the minutes to identify each man by his color. The Reverend James Lynch rose and moved that the color of each delegate's hair be also included in the minutes.

The convention did the best it could under the continual provocations from the streets and newspapers of Jackson and from the hostility of the new commanding general, Alvan C. Gillam of Tennessee, who disliked the entire business, did not believe Negroes should have the vote, and withheld all advice and protection.

The convention may have been composed largely of ignorant, poor and quarrelsome men (fights on the floor broke out frequently)—"baboons and mongrelized human beings," the local newspaper called them—but they put together a modern instrument of government under which Mississippi lived for twenty-two years. Property qualifications for voting were eliminated. Free travel was made a man's natural right; passes, the old badge of Negro slavery, were abolished. An unsegregated public school was required "for all children between the ages of five and twenty-one." (During the first year of free education, a long two years after the convention, 3500 teachers in

87

3,000 schools taught 66,000 students. Public education had more spent on it than all the other agencies put together.)

It was the white delegates who demanded that men who had aided the Confederacy be forbidden the vote. They attempted to disfranchise twenty thousand of the most influential men in the state. The Negroes opposed this, demanding and getting an unrestricted franchise.

It took them a hundred and fifteen harried days to accomplish these things however, and chaos broke out immediately afterward.

As soon as the convention adjourned the delegates had to begin a fight for the life of the constitution. Governor Humphreys so sedulously, consistently, and resourcefully opposed any election to implement the constitution that the military authority ordered him to give up his office. General Adelbert Ames of Maine was appointed Acting Governor. General Humphreys refused to yield. Soldiers carried him out.

It was obvious that the fight against the constitution was well planned. While the convention was sitting, another convention, entirely white, had been called in Jackson by Democrats. Their platform was opposition to the "nefarious design of the Republican party in Congress to place the white men of the southern states under the governmental control of their late slaves, degrading the Caucasian race. [This] is a crime against the civilization of the age . . . We therefore call upon the people of Mississippi to vindicate alike the superiority of their race over the Negro and their political power, and to maintain constitutional liberty."

They set to work to implement their program as soon as the constitutional convention was over. They concentrated their efforts on the black counties—the plantation area—where intimidation filled the air.

Here Negro field hands and white farmers were assured

that they would be evicted and "experience the everlasting enmity of those upon whom they depend for employment" if they did not vote against the constitution and for the Democrats. "There is now an awful gulf yawning before you. If you abandon the people with whom you have ever lived and who now invite you to their protection in the future, you cast your destiny with an enemy between whom and us there is eternal war."

Yet artfulness was employed as well as threats. At Democratic rallies, planters and members of the Klan invited field hands and mechanics to sit on the platform with them. They reminded them in their speeches of the old paternalism under slavery. This concern for controlled voting extended as far as a picnic, with all good Democrats sitting in separate blocs together.

The Republicans took an extremely cautious position. Not one Negro was nominated for a state or county office.

When election day came, Democratic officials ostentatiously wrote down the names of those who used the distinctive Republican ballot, whether they were Negroes or whites. The Union troops had been given their orders by General Gillam, and they carried out their instructions to the letter, warning the Negroes of terrible retribution if they voted for the constitution. Some of the soldiers openly electioneered for the Democrats as the Negroes drew near the polls. In the larger towns, General Gillam ordered segregated polling booths.

The constitution lost by sixty-three thousand votes—but the vote *for* it was a surprise. Fifty-six thousand voters had eaten of the metaphorical picnics and then cast their votes for free schools and justice for all.

Even the Democrats conceded that fraud and violence had been essential to keep Mississippi still out of the Union. The white Republicans were thoroughly discouraged. The handful of Negro leaders in the state urged another constitutional convention in which some technique of working with the planters, short of being swallowed alive, could be evolved. In Mississippi this seemed the only realistic means of participating in the future.

South Carolina, which like Mississippi had a Negro majority, was at the other end of the spectrum. The plantations here were old and settled, with a strong element of paternalism. The large core of free Negroes had acted as a leaven—there were ten thousand in 1860, most of them able to read and write—and some degree of education was not unknown to the slave. In Charleston, free Negroes had run secret schools for slaves.

At Johnson's inauguration, Charleston had celebrated by opening the existing schools to all children, Negro as well as white—and twenty-five of the forty-two teachers were colored. A correspondent for the *New York Tribune* wrote, "In the playgrounds white and black boys joined in the same sports as they do in the public streets; and there can be no doubt that now that this great step has been made, all the prejudice against equal educational advantages will speedily vanish, and indeed it is the veriest hypocrisy in the city where very old families have aided in obliterating all the complexional distinctions by mingling their blood with that of the slaves."

On January 14, 1868, the constitutional convention met in Charleston. Earlier party conventions had to some extent prepared the way for it. South Carolina white men were sharply divided about policy and this attitude led to three parties: the Union Republican, a liberal catch-all, headed by former South Carolina Governor Orr, who was willing to accept the Reconstruction Acts and work with the Negroes; an ambiguously liberal Democratic party headed by Wade Hampton, who did not oppose the acts openly but intended to use them to dominate the Negro; and conservative Democrats led by Benjamin F. Perry, who attacked the Hampton position by crying, "Why, oh, why, my southern nigger-worshippers, will you grope your

90

way through this worse than Egyptian darkness? Why not cease this crawling on your bellies and assume the upright form of men?"

The delegates to the constitutional convention were a unique group of men. They came from the hill country, from the rice plantations, from the fields, from the cities. Never before in modern history had such an assemblage been seen. One hundred and twenty-four delegates arrived and seventy-six were Negroes.

The white delegates were both aristocrats and poor whites. One had helped pull down the United States flag at Fort Sumter, another had been a slave trader.

The unfriendly said this convention would be "the maddest, most unscrupulous and infamous revolution in history." But the "Negro bedlam" did not develop. Even the newspapers commented on the extreme seriousness of the Negro delegates, whose only aggressive act was to expel a reporter who called them "the ringed, striped and streaked convention." There was purpose and economy of action, and much of this was due to the remarkable caliber of some of the Negro delegates.

South Carolina had long had a comparitively large class of educated Negroes—despised and outcast but owning themselves and some property. Francis L. Cardozo came from such a family. Born in Charleston in 1837, he had gone to school till he was twelve years old, and had then been apprenticed to a carpenter. By the time he was twenty-one, he had saved up enough money to make his way to Glasgow, Scotland, to study for the ministry. He stayed four years at the University of Glasgow, working at carpentry or any employment to pay his tuition, and winning prizes in Latin and Greek. In a competitive examination among graduates of four colleges, he won a scholarship of one thousand dollars which brought him to London and more advanced study. When he returned to the United States in 1864, he became pastor to the Temple Street Congregational Church in New Haven, Connecticut. As soon as the war was over, Cardozo had returned to South Carolina as principal of a normal school for colored students, and he was still principal when elected to the convention.

The Reverend Richard Harvey Cain was a delegate. He had been born in Virginia of free parents, been educated in Ohio, and entered the ministry as a Methodist. For four years he was pastor of a Brooklyn church. In 1865, he was sent South as a church missionary. Churches seemed to bloom wherever he walked. He became immediately active in politics and in 1866 edited a Republican newspaper in Charleston.

Robert Smalls was a delegate. He had been born a slave in South Carolina in 1839. He learned to read and write after a fashion, and his master, who moved to Charleston, hired him out to work as a rigger and to learn the sailing of ships. Presently he was transferred to the *Planter,* a small transport steamer that carried supplies along the coast. Smalls remained as pilot with the ship until one night in May 1862, when only the Negro crew was aboard, Smalls proposed to deliver the ship to the Union navy, and all but two of the crew agreed. The others waited only long enough to bring wives and children aboard, and shortly after midnight crept out under the guns of Sumter.

The North made him a hero. He remained as pilot of the *Planter* all through the war. When the little ship was put out of commission in 1866, Smalls returned home. He was a zealous, intelligent man, who communicated his enthusiasm.

Jonathan J. Wright was born of free parents in Pennsylvania. He was now twenty-eight years old. He had saved enough money to go to the University at Ithaca, New York, and presently studied law. The American Missionary Society sent him to South Carolina in 1865, to organize schools He returned home after the passage of the first Civil Rights law so that he could pass the bar examinations of Pennsylvania. (He had been refused a legal examination in 1865.) For two years he was stationed at Beaufort, S. C., as General Howard's legal adviser on refugees and freedmen. He came to the convention as a delegate from Beaufort. "Although he lisped he was a good speaker."

Robert Elliott was twenty-six. He had been born in Massachusetts of West Indian parents. He had gone to a private school in Boston, and then to an academy in London where he had studied for three years. At the end of that time, he went to Eton. He graduated from Eton with high honors in 1859, and remained in England studying law. When he returned to the United States he chose South Carolina for his home, and newspaper editorship for his profession. He was editor of the *Charleston Leader* when he was elected to the convention.

Robert DeLarge had been born in Aiken, North Carolina. A slave, he had taught himself to read and write. With a great interest in politics, he enjoyed picking his way through the staggering intricacies of rival groups and interracial tensions. When he ran successfully for Congress, many whites voted for him in preference to his white rival. He died when he was thirty-two.

Beverly Nash had been a slave until 1865. He could still barely read or write. But he was shrewd, scrupulously honest, clear-headed in argument, extremely quick in debate, and considered, even by his Democratic enemies, the ablest Negro in South Carolina. They frankly said they wished he were a Democrat.

Land and education were once again the primary concerns of a convention. These were the issues which spoke directly to every delegate and voter. They did not need to be explained. They were fundamental to every other issue. Without them there would not be a state.

These delegates spent many days discussing property. They offered many shrewd evaluations of what it meant— for most of these men had *been* property.

Cardozo, who had not been a slave, opposed confiscation, preferring a homestead law which would break up the plantation system into many small farms "for citizens irrespective of color."

Race discimination was attacked from many angles and an amendment proposed that "Distinction on account of race or color in any case whatever shall be prohibited, and all classes of citizens . . . shall enjoy all common, equal and political privileges." The rights of women were taken into account—even the possibility of women voting was suggested—and the property of married women was protected.

The discussion of education was detailed and prolonged. Everyone agreed that children should be taught until the age of twenty-one. The public school system would be unsegregated, but for those who could not bring themselves to associate with Negroes, and for those Negroes who preferred "separate schools until some of the present prejudice against their race is removed," private schools were allowed. The deaf, dumb, and blind were not forgotten. For the first time education was being visualized in its totality.

In the interval before the money could be raised, a Negro member proposed that the Freedmen's Bureau be asked to continue its schools until a Board of Education could establish an efficient educational system.

Public education at public expense for all children was, in the South, a Negro innovation. A public system of education—for whites only—had received more lip service than support in the past. Many state legislatures had discussed elaborate plans at session after session, and schools for the indigent were frequently spoken of, but with rare exceptions they remained merely hope and expectation.

The decisions of the constitutional convention required a great deal of money. Taxation of a war-ruined economy had to be faced, and perhaps the only way it could be faced by financially naïve men was to vote a budget. It was voted in a spirit of faith.

South Carolina was a state which had been badly wracked by war. The convention recommended an over-hauling of local and judicial administration, a Court of Probate to be established in each county, and justices of the peace used with a broader effectiveness. Judges were to be elected, not appointed. Imprisonment for debt was abolished; so were property qualifications for voting or holding office.

The convention was harmonious although everyone took part at full voice, and most resolutions were passed unanimously by white and Negro delegates.

Democrats of South Carolina made their pronouncement as soon as the convention had finished. The constitution "was the work of sixty-odd Negroes, many of them ignorant and depraved, together with fifty white men, outcasts of Northern society and Southern renegades, betrayers of their race and country."

A white woman expressed incredulity. "You might as well teach your horse or mule to read as teach these niggers." This was repeated to a colored delegate, who had urged that education be compulsory, and he sent her a message. "In proportion to the education of the people, so is there progress in civilization."

The North Carolina convention also met on January 14. In Raleigh, thirteen Negro delegates met with sixteen whites called "carpetbaggers" and one hundred and two called "scalawags."

North Carolina had had considerable individuality during slavery. Thirty thousand free Negroes had possessed and used the vote until 1835. One of the famous schools in the South for aristocratic white boys had been conducted by a Negro, John Chavis, who had been educated at Princeton.

It was North Carolina which had received the first

blessings of Johnson's amnesty six weeks after the end of the war, when the new President pardoned William W. Holden and appointed him provisional governor. Holden was a North Carolinian with liberal ideas, but in the elections of 1866 he lost to an archconservative. He then became the leader of the Republicans in the state, and the North Carolina Negroes sent a petition to Congress expressing their support.

In this present constitutional convention Holden played a large part. Among the Negroes, the Reverend James H. Harris, born in North Carolina, educated in Ohio; and the Reverend James Walker Hood, born in Pennsylvania and sent South as a missionary by the African Zion Church, dominated many of the committees.

Segregation in schools, intermarriage, and the holding of state offices by Negroes were the most controversial issues. Universal male suffrage, free and unsegregated public schools, abolition of property qualifications for the vote, and provisions for vagrants, orphans, and other unfortunates were agreed on without too much confusion. The rest was left in abeyance.

North Carolina could have been a model state in this vast experiment in living. There was enough flexibility within its history to make it possible. Why this did not happen is hard to say. The real struggle in North Carolina had little to do with the Negro; the real struggle lay between the white men, and it had three prongs. Many white Northerners had come into the state—a larger number than in any other southern state. Their control was feared by the landed gentry and also by the large body of nonslaveholding whites who, historically, had possessed considerable power in North Carolina. None of the three groups wished to yield the fruit which they saw growing in the future, and the Negro had to fend for himself as best he could.

The planters gave a characteristic opinion of the convention and its delegates: "Ethiopian minstrelry, ham radicalism in is glory, baboons, monkeys, mules, and other jackasses."

Florida had a large Negro population which was increased by the hundreds of Negro soldiers stationed there. It also had a large and powerful group of northern white men who struggled diligently for state control. It was a southern state in its loyalties and attitudes, northern in its expectations and hustle.

Forty-six delegates came to the state convention on January 20. Eighteen were Negroes. The most remarkable Negro was Jonathan Gibbs. He was now thirty-seven years old. Born in Pennsylvania of free parents, he had graduated from Dartmouth College. The Presbyterian church claimed him as a minister and sent him South in 1865 to organize churches and schools among the freedmen. He reached Florida in 1867 and almost immediately acquired great influence among the Negroes. White people on the whole did not like him, but they agreed somewhat sourly that he was "the most cultured member of the convention." His manners were excellent and his mind very quick in debate. In the first new Florida government he was to be secretary of state.

Money concerned this convention more than almost anything else. There was exactly $500 in the state treasury. The peculiar characteristic of the Florida convention was the intense rivalry between the natural-born Floridian and the Northerner who claimed it as his state. The rocking fight left the Negroes badly exposed, and Gibbs is credited with having steered them past many flying fists.

After two weeks the convention split in half. The Radical Republicans, with one vote majority, remained in Tallahassee, and the Johnson rump withdrew twenty-five miles to form a rival convention. Both drew up constitutions. The Johnson rump broke into the legislative hall at midnight announcing that they were the true representatives of the state. The commanding general, Meade, obliged the two groups to yield their hegemony and the constitution of the Johnson men was accepted. But it was such an odd, unsatisfying document that, in Congress, Sumner tried to prevent the admission of Florida. He did not succeed. "The ensuing tumult cannot be understood unless one keeps carefully in mind just what was taking place. The planters were encouraging lawlessness and inciting the Negroes to make extravagant demands for equality in order to embarrass the carpetbaggers and excite the poor whites. The carpetbaggers and northern capitalists were seeking to get rid of Governor Harrison Reed, and bribing white and black members of the legislature in order to get through social legislation for capital. The Negroes were trying to find a program of labor legislation which would help the poor; Reed was playing capital, labor and planters against each other, and in the midst of these contradictory and opposing forces, the state staggered on," writes Dr. DuBois.

The railways of Florida, half complete, were bankrupt, schools had come to a complete halt for lack of funds, there were no social agencies, no poor houses, penitentiaries, or even a lockup.

During January, Alabama discussed a constitution. There were ninety white men, thirty-one of whom were Northerners; eighteen of those, members of the Freedmen's Bureau. The anonymity of these white liberals is tantalizing. It would be immensely enriching if we knew something about them—although perhaps their status as Freedmen's Bureau agents makes an enlightening statement.

Eighteen Negroes were present. One of them, James Thomas Rapier, was thirty-one years old. He had been born in Florence, Alabama; his father was not only free but wealthy—wealthy enough to provide a tutor for his son. However, he went to Canada for the bulk of his education and was admitted to the bar. He came back to Alabama in

1865 and became a prosperous cotton planter, at the same time showing an interest in politics. Before long, he would be on his way to Washington as a congressman.

Jeremiah Haralson was a vigorous contrast. An extremely black man (which filled him with pride), born a slave in Georgia, burly, shrewd, and poorly educated, he became a power in the state. The Negroes trusted him; the white people respected him; he never pulled down his flag. He was far more inclined to work with white people than Rapier, and his constant fight was for racial goodwill in Alabama—with schools for all! He too went to Congress.

The *Independent Monitor* of Tuscaloosa greeted the convention: "Cultivate a Christian disposition toward all but nigger worshippers whom the Holy Apostles would have considered human monstrosities had they lived in their day." A day of fasting was also appointed, with prayers that the state should be delivered "from the horrors of Negro domination." This must have fallen oddly on the ears of Confederate officers who were members of the new legislature.

A Negro named Alfred Gray stood up on the courthouse steps in Uniontown, Alabama, to answer such sentiments. "This Constitution—I came here to talk for it. I am not afraid to fight for it, and I will fight for it till hell freezes over. I, afraid to fight for my rights? No, I may go to hell, but the White man shall go there with me! ... You hear a good deal about social equality and black and white children going to school together. Well, ain't that right? We pay our $1.50—so make them pay tax on the land that you cleared and which you have the best right to. Then send all to school together ... Boys, now I want you to hear. Everyone come in and bring your guns and stand up for your rights ... We'll fight till we die and go to hell together—or we'll carry this constitution!"

The franchise and intermarriage interested the convention more than other subjects. The Alabama whites wanted the Confederates disfranchised again, the Negroes insisted on the vote for all. The Alabama whites wanted intermarriage prohibited; a Negro delegate said it was against the Civil Rights Bill to interfere. A Negro from Dallas County made a motion, which was passed, that Negroes be paid wages retroactively from the day of Emancipation in 1863 to the end of the war in 1865.

In the end sixteen of the white delegates refused to sign the constitution and protested aganist the convention's refusal to establish segregated schools.

The Democrats did all they could, in a separate Democratic convention, to defeat the constitution.

Texas, which held its convention in February, had no problems of bankruptcy or broken roads or shattered bridges—it was prospering mightily, in fact. Its problems were rival Democratic controls. However, the election went quietly and a large vote was cast. Ninety members came to the convention, including nine Negroes. Several of them were very competent but none of them made any special impression on the state. A committee "on lawlessness and violence" reported that 509 whites and 486 Negroes had been killed from 1865 to 1868. More than 90 percent of the killers were white men.

The struggle for voting was a serious one, but at length the right was extended to Negroes. A good school system was set up, with money from the sale of public lands going into the fund.

The convention never really adjourned nor was the constitution ever submitted to a formal vote. But everyone seemed to understand the situation, and by 1870, Texas was a part of the Union again.

Louisiana was the last of the seceded states to meet. The convention sat down in New Orleans in March and once again the issues turned on controlling the vote. The Democrats believed they had to win in Louisiana in order to win in the country at large. They were not all agreed on how to do this. The more moderate voices urged that some accommodation with Negro suffrage was inevitable and the Democrats had best turn their attention toward ways of controlling that vote.

General James Longstreet, whose devotion to the Confederacy could hardly be doubted, took a further and remarkable step. Two open letters from him were published in the *New Orleans Republican*.

"I shall be happy to work under any measure that promises to bring the glory of peace and goodwill toward men," he wrote. "The sword has decided in favor of the North and what they claim as principles cease to be principles and are become law. It is therefore our duty to abandon ideas that are obsolete and conform to the requirements of law. . . . It becomes us to insist that suffrage be extended in all the states and fully tested."

He spoke for decent and honorable men, and many of those decent men were about to sit down in a new amity, seeing black as a color of God, and able to legislate in a common good.

White advisers had vigorously urged that the Negro delegates to the convention be carefully chosen by the voters. Forty-nine Negro delegates were on hand and forty-nine whites. Among the Negroes were not only representatives from the upland plantations which shared with Mississippi the same rawness and desolation, but also urban Negroes of property and education.

New Orleans, with its mixture of races, its system of common-law mulatto wives, had more educated and wealthy Negroes than any other city in the South. But outside of New Orleans, there was not a single road with a hard surface. There was only one canal, and communication was poor, for mails were erratic and the telegraphic system exceedingly limited. New Orleans itself had only four paved streets; the rest were a quagmire in the rainy season and a misery of dust in the dry season. Lotteries, licensed gambling parlors, and brothels provided a large part of the city income. It was freely said that the police force was made up of men with criminal records. This was a state full of contrasts, and the delegates reflected them all.

For example, Oscar Dunn had been born a slave, had escaped and bought both his freedom and his education. He proved to be a very powerful man and for a time virtually ran the state, yet even the Democrats called him "incorruptible."

P. B. S. Pinchback was the son of a Mississippi planter and the Negro woman who had borne him ten children. He had been educated in Ohio and commanded a Negro regiment during the war. He was almost white in complexion, and although extremely shrewd, seemed to many Louisiana Negroes more interested in picking his way through the infinite ramifications of state politics than of giving a positive leadership. However, his reputation became national and he was a very powerful man.

Four Negroes and five white delegates made up the committee to draft the constitution. Their points of difference were included in minority and majority reports.

The white men wished to disfranchise all Confederates, the Negroes protested, "as we are now and ever have been advocates of universal suffrage," but they agreed to a restriction on officeholding. The white delegates wanted a strict regulation of labor and wages. The Negroes wished no restrictions and insisted that children bound out into virtual slavery by apprenticeship laws be returned to their parents. White delegates favored a free education (the state had inherited an excellent public school system from the Union occupation). The Negroes wanted this extended and amplified so that there was "at least one free public school in every parish, to be provided for by public taxation, and with no distinction as to race and sex." They also asked for a state university with six faculties.

The constitution took care of both points of view. The

price of manual labor was not fixed; Confederate leaders could neither vote nor hold offices; schools in every parish, and a university, were assured.

According to the planters this constitution "Was the work of the lowest and most corrupt body of men ever assembled in the South. It was the work of ignorant Negroes cooperating with a gang of white adventurers, strangers to our interests and our sentiments."

So state by state it went, fundamental rights the keystones. All the states were torn by factionalism, violent infighting, and armed opposition, so that the embattled Negroes and their friends had to watch all ways at once. Voting on the constitutions was imperative if the state was to return to the Union. Many conservatives felt that they should remain quiet until that last step had been taken, but others had kept their battles raging while the conventions sat, and rolled up even heavier artillery the moment the delegates dispersed.

In North and South Carolina, Georgia, Florida, and Arkansas the constitutions were narrowly ratified. As each state went back into the Union, the old-fashioned voters insisted that the constitution did not reflect their thinking. "These documents, framed by ignorance, malevolence and partisanship," Claude Bowers, a southern historian recorded later, "sounded the death-knell of civilization in the South."

Yet an interesting fact emerges about that "partisanship": in the conventions where the white delegates were in the majority, the amendments and acts directed at the total disfranchisement of the planters were far more stringent than in the states where the Negroes held the majority.

THE REPUBLICANS in Washington, watching the conventions as they struggled noisily into life, aware of the passion and power of a new society, had agreed upon inpeachment.

On February 22, 1868, the House met in a special session. The debate went on for two days. Late in the afternoon of the 24th, with the snow falling heavily outside and the gas lights flaring in the House, Stevens hopelessly ill, arose.

He could barely get to his feet. He had spent most of the debate lying on a couch in an anteroom and yet he seemed to control the entire network of the House.

In the House Chamber there was absolute silence. In the galleries, dark faces watched with anxiety, for every Negro knew that no one had fought so consistently for his rights—unless it was Sumner, that other great fighter in the Senate. And Sumner said of Stevens on this day, "I doubt if words were ever delivered to more effect."

Stevens' thin tough body stood erect for a moment, his voice as familiar as the voice of their fathers. But after a moment he swayed. After five minutes his voice left him. With a gesture of apology he handed his speech to the clerk of the House and sank back into his chair.

The burden of the speech was simple: Who represented the will of the people? An elected Congress or a President who by his manifold vetoes frustrated their will? Johnson had used the veto twenty-three times. This constituted, in time of crisis, a crime of incalculable magnitude.

The vote to bring Johnson to trial was a strict party vote.

Stevens was then carried to the Senate Chamber in his armchair, followed by a delegation from the House.

"In obedience to the order of the House of Representatives," he said, exerting his voice for a moment, "we appear before you in the name of the House and of all the people of the United States. We do impeach Andrew Johnson, President of the United States, of high crimes and misdemeanors in office; and we further inform the Senate that the House of Representatives will in due time exhibit articles against him . . ."

The Senate was organized as a Court, and on March 13, 1868, faced the defendant. Chief Justice Chase presided, and Johnson had several able lawyers as his counsel.

The trial lasted for two months. Much of the time it was carried on in flaming anger, all the sins of Reconstruction brandished on both sides. The bloody shirt of a white man who had attempted to vote in Mississippi was waved against Johnson. Charges and countercharges were flung both in the Senate and in the halls of the Capitol. Trickery was assumed on both sides; even during the trial it was hinted that money would secure an acquittal.

Stevens was silent during the trial. He rose only when the final arguments were being offered, and then he merely enumerated Johnson's hostile acts denying citizenship to the Negro.

Johnson was acquitted by a single vote. When the acquittal was announced, "the whole aspect of the House was that of an assemblage smitten with news of a great calamity," The *New York World* reported.

Two days after the acquittal, the Republican convention met in Chicago. Only one name was seriously considered: Ulysses S. Grant.

Grant had his own special virtues and weaknesses. Like many soldiers, he hated war. He felt great compassion for the South over which a war had ripped its way. He had seen the blighted fields and ruined houses. And he knew that the white Confederates were not the only sufferers. He knew that the Negro bore a double burden. But he had the cautious conviction that most Northerners wished to withold the vote from the Negro until some hypothetical amount of education had destroyed the smell of slavery.

The Republican platform tried to straddle the issue: Congressional guarantees of suffrage for the Negro where the Republicans needed the votes—in the South—and a genuflection to states' rights in the North.

It was a year promising such shift and change that men's allegiances floated back and forth. Johnson, who had been principal speaker at the Jackson Day Meeting in Washington, had dreams of being the Democratic nominee. So had Chief Justice Chase, a melancholic figure; he had been an Abolitionist in the days before the war, a Radical Republican in the days after the war, but his fear of military rule in the South was stronger than his practical knowlege that Negro citizenship could be protected in no other way. Conservative pressure on him grew so sharp that he was forced to say publicly that the Supreme Court had no intention of declaring the Reconstruction Acts unconstitutional. With the end of Johnson's trial, he turned more and more to the Democrats, for Republicans like Horace Greeley openly charged him with having swung the acquittal.

The Democrats held their national convention in July in Philadelphia. The convention was entirely southern in its sentiments, and it included most of the popular issues in its discussions—protective tariffs, currency control, Negro suffrage. It did not come out flatly against votes for the Negro, but insisted that suffrage was a problem for the states.

General Wade Hampton of South Carolina was there, a man whose power would, in less than ten years, become formidable. General Nathan Forrest, still Grand Master of the Klans, was there. Howell Cobb, former governor and former senator from Georgia, was there; and also Robert Toombs, who had exerted an almost unparalleled power in the slave oligarchy when he was senator from Georgia. His self-imposed exile in Europe was broken for this convention and he set old echoes ringing again. "I regret nothing in the past but the dead and the failure. I am ready today to use the best means I can command to establish the principles for which I fought."

Johnson was angry and humiliated when the nomination went to Horatio Seymour, wartime governor of New York, "the embodiment of copperheadism" as Horace Greeley called him. The vice-presidential candidate, Blair of Missouri, demanded that the new governments in the South be broken by force as soon as the Democrats resumed power.

The Democrats, representing nearly 50 percent of the northern voters, would undoubtedly win if they could control the new votes in the South. The 1868 election was so crucial that the whole course of Reconstruction depended on the outcome. If the Republicans failed to speak convincingly for northern business, their tenuous hold on power would probably be broken. But northern business, filled with the afflatus of unmeasured opportunities and with a residual antislavery impulse, was convinced that disaster would follow if the South were returned to the past.

The Negro had now become a percentage figure—12.7 of the population. When he got education in his head and money in his pocket he was not to be overlooked.

The Negroes were courted. Even the Democrats courted them. In South Carolina, at a meeting of the Democratic party, Beverly Nash, the black former slave and very shrewd legislator, was asked to sit on the platform with Wade Hampton. Nash was no Democrat, but he was becoming a power in the state, and Hampton in his speech expounded the doctrine of a common destiny. Overnight an astonishing number of old-fashioned men found the principle of Negro political rights extremely attractive, and attempted to make a strength out of weakness by appealing for a common stand against the "usurpers" from the North.

In Alabama, the Democrats assured the Negroes "that the whites of the South" wished them to "remain free and possess their rights for all time . . . Let every white man and honest black man in the state fall into the Democratic ranks and make a crushing charge upon the shattered cohorts of scalawags and carpetbaggers."

This double language was not lost on the Negroes. "Scalawags" were those southern whites who worked with them, and "carpetbaggers" was an umbrella term for all those who had come from the North: school teachers, Freedmen's agents, business men, rogues, and honest investors.

In March, the Republicans had formed their first state organization in the South. A large mass meeting had been held in Charleston, with bands and torchlight parades and wonderfully eager new citizens. They had listened to the reading of the Republican platform to a chorus of clashing cymbals and ear-splitting shouts. It called for the abolition of large estates, education for all children, white or colored, protection of Negro voters.

The Mississippi Republican convention was made up of one-third Negroes. The Union Leagues promised to work for the education of the voters, and the delegates bound themselves to "keep step with all the progressive political reforms of the age."

The Republicans appealed to "the laboring masses" in Virginia and Florida. If this was taken too literally to mean "Negroes," their true intention was clarified. We "do not desire to deprive the laboring white man of any rights or privileges which they now enjoy but do propose to extend those rights and privileges."

A former slaveowner in Florida lost his temper at one of these meetings. "We know what you are talking and doing. You are drilling over the country . . . What rights do you want? The property of the whites? You intend to fight for it do you? . . . Whenever you get ready, strike the blow, and you will see the hell of ruin which your radical teachers have brought you."

Steady-functioning state governments were essential before the Persidential elections in the fall. In Louisiana, the legislature convened in June. H. C. Warmoth was governor. He was twenty-six years old, born in Illinois, though he claimed not a drop of northern blood ran in his veins. Everyone liked him—no one trusted him—and they were right on both counts. His lieutenant governor was Oscar Dunn, who signed the three main legal codes which have, to this day, remained basic to the state.

There were seven Negroes in the State Senate, all of whom had been freemen. Among them was P. B. S. Pinchback, so white that his identification as a Negro was his own choice. He did not have the idealism of Dunn but he had his own verve and his own integrity.

In all, forty-nine Negroes sat in the Louisiana legislature and eighty-eight whites.

In July, South Carolina met to govern. Eighty-four Negroes and seventy-three whites made up the legislature. Francis Cardozo became secretary of state. A Freedmen's Bureau commissioner, Robert K. Scott of Pennsylvania, became governor. South Carolina had, without question, the most informed and educated Negro legislators of any southern state. Robert Elliott was a first-rate lawyer and speaker. Robert Cain was not only a journalist, but eventually a bishop. Robert DeLarge had been a Freedmen's Bureau agent. Richard H. Gleaves had been a probate judge in Pennsylvania. Samuel Lee, who became Speaker, was a free Negro of South Carolina and self-taught as a lawyer. Stephen Swailes had been a Union soldier and a school teacher. But Robert Smalls was probably the most popular of all. The story went around of a colloquy between two admirers. "I tell you, Smalls is the greatest man in the world." "Yes, he's great, but not the greatest man." "Who is greater than Smalls?" "Why, Jesus Christ." "Oh, Smalls is young yet."

The Fourteenth Amendment was promptly ratified by South Carolina—and by North Carolina when its legislature convened in July. The General Assembly in Raleigh was required by its constitution to provide immediate free schools for all children between the ages of six and twenty-one. A Freedmen's Bureau report showed that already twenty-six thousand freedmen were going to private schools—those shacks and tree arbors and churches—maintained by religious groups.

In July, the Alabama assembly met, with twenty-six Negroes in the House and one lone fellow in the Senate, and by the end of the summer, Arkansas, Georgia, and Florida were also ready to come into the Union on the basis of their new constitutions.

The new constitutions were automatically attacked, whatever their merits. The legislators had not only to learn administration, how to weld an organization which would fight for the measures, but how to defend themselves from ideological as well as physical blows. This required endless skill and resourcefulness, since the army was required to be as inconspicuous as possible, intervening only if matters became intolerable. And "intolerable" for reasons of expediency had a limited meaning.

The Union Leagues had been strengthening themselves all through these months, for the federal troops were thinly spaced over the South, and were not to be trusted blindly, as Mississippi had discovered. The Leagues would have to bear the brunt of the fall elections.

League meetings were held once a week in schools or churches. They were generally guarded by armed men, with sentries set to give the alarm. The white men who were members were heroes, for the Negroes did not wholly trust them, and the white conservatives detested them. But they were an indispensable sinew of freedom.

The Leagues were semisecret to protect themselves. They had their emblems—the Altar, the Holy Bible, the Declaration of Independence, the Union flag, the sword and the ballot box, the sickle and the anvil.

As the Republican parties grew stronger, the Leagues worked closely with them, but it was the Leagues which provided the political education. This education was sometimes attained through raw and imflammatory speeches, at other times through quiet discussions of essential needs. League members were disciplined to the avoidance of trouble; they were schooled for the purposes of defense. It is safe to make a categoric statement: without them the free vote could not have been exercised in the South at this time.

At Talladega, Alabama, two thousand Negroes paraded through the streets to join white Alabamans at a great mass meeting in the courthouse square where speeches were made supporting the Republican party and demanding a good public school system. At Uniontown, another large meeting of whites and Negroes protested any effort to keep them apart and called on landless whites, artisans, mechanics to cooperate in the Leagues and the Republican party.

All through that summer the Leagues held organized meetings of Negroes and whites. Negroes and whites paraded together. They shared the same slogans, "Bread, wages, and schools."

Thaddeus Stevens was now so ill, he seldom left his home. Yet his power remained in some remarkable way undimmed. Cabinet members, ambassadors, senators, newspaper correspondents—even the public—came to his small brick house on South B Street.

His own state of Pennsylvania had refused to give the vote to the Negro, and his passionate concern was now for a Fifteenth Amendment to insure constitutional voting rights. He talked about it constantly. He had a modicum of faith in Grant, although he was outraged when the Republican Convention did not have the courage to endorse universal suffrage. A political realist, he believed that the height of Republican radicalism had been passed and that unless the Negro was buttressed on all sides by the law, he would be undone. The Democratic National Convention, with its Copperheads and southern planters in control, depressed him unspeakably.

And Mississippi, where the new constitution had been defeated, lay like a pall over him. He was profoundly aware that the new governments were strange hybrids, representing social change and opportunism in equal parts. The Negroes held numerical advantage in only two states: South Carolina and Mississippi. In only four states did they hold the balance of power.

Since they were also despised, ignorant and penniless, their ballot could be merely a piece of paper without the Leagues, and if the government in Washington decided to withhold the support of federal troops, the polling places would become battlefields. Without support of every kind, education, goodwill, law, economic power, their days were numbered.

Too many of the white men who voted with them were transients—Northerners who might leave at any time. The new South had been thrust into power by desperate necessity without plan or preparation. How could it have been otherwise unless the entire moral and social antecedents of the South had been miraculously expunged?

Perhaps the Negro should have been ruthlessly wakened from his dream of owning land. Held in the dream he was unwilling and unable to find other means to insure his independence. Yet what would have been those means? No old-fashioned man was going to sell him land—even when he had the money to buy it—as long as the planters were determined to hold laborers to the plantation system. Was the only possible chance to be found in such a violent economic change that the whole American system would be affected by a democratic revolution a hundred years ahead of its time: or was an esoteric mystery the answer? Must dignity grow out of the naked soul, out of the Negro's new evaluation of himself? Probably a combination of both was involved: social change linked with metaphysics, each having its profound element of truth.

Out of anguish and poverty, out of ignorance and subjection, the disinherited, the cast-off, were obliged to find their own identities in a clawing, stinging, hating world where the man in power was concerned only for himself. The miracle remains that they succeeded to a degree unseen before in history.

By July 28, 1868, the Fourteenth Amendment had been ratified by enough states to become law. But already its inadequacies were painfully clear.

Three weeks later, Thaddeus Stevens died. Two Negro clergymen were with him, as well as the fair-skinned Negro woman who had cared for him for twenty years and whom, it was believed, he had loved with all his heart.

His body was laid in a Negro cemetery. Above his head was written: "I repose in this quiet and secluded spot, not from any natural preference for solitude but finding other cemeteries limited as to race by charter rules, I have chosen this that I might illustrate in my death the principles which I advocated through a long life: the Equality of Man before his Creator."

Sumner said, "Politician, calculator, time-server, stand aside: A hero statesman passes to his reward."

The loss of Stevens was grievous. He had a genius for leadership. Although his hand was iron, he used it with the adroitness of a great politician. He had been called by southern historians "a malignant cancer," "a horrible old man" whose policy was "simply a set of hates strung together in a pattern."

Indeed he hated ignorance. He hated caste. He hated inequality. He believed that no one can learn self-government without the rights of self-government.

The Civil War was fought over the question of human dignity: this is what Carl Sandburg suggests. Stevens knew that human dignity must be nurtured until it was strong enough to care for itself. He believed that the dignity of white men and colored was interdependent, that the degradation of Negroes did not contribute to the dignity of the whites.

All the evils of Reconstruction have been laid at his feet. But he was obliged to work with what he had, and what did he have? Chaos, greed, men trained immemorially to leadership determined to perpetuate the past; no time in which to season and teach those who, emerging out of brutalized anonymity, must now give substance to the immense truths of self-government. A desperate kind of trust had to become a policy: a trust that man had the power to know what was right and to act with courage so that he might, through trial and failure, stumble into his kingdom.

When all the angry words have been exchanged, all the vulgar and pusillanimous things said about Stevens, the truth emerges: without him, no hope would have been given root, no guidelines laid for today.

He had no successor. One of his contemporaries had said that if his skull were cracked, the brains of the Republican party would run out.

Sumner was a great man, but Sumner raised impenetrable barriers by the adamantine nature of his own moral positions and then had to waste great energy breaking through the massive hostility he had created. But for the next five years, Sumner rises like a mountain.

The Presidential campaign started about the time of Stevens' death. It was a wild, disorderly, shouting campaign, in which new power, new wealth, new-days-ahead were hollered and hallooed in every town and village. It signaled the breakdown of standards of behavior, even of common decency and honor. Land and money speculators seemed to have seized the government.

The railroad scandals were blossoming (federal, state, and local governments assumed three-fifths of the cost of railroads and then handed them over to private owners for individual profit), the land scandals were blooming (338,000 square miles of land was snatched from home-steaders and given to land speculators). Boss Tweed had begun his extraordinary speculations which would amount to a steal of seventy-five million dollars of public money, and bribery was already accepted as a normal form of control in Congress and in business.

All through the campaign, votes were bought and sold as commodities. In Philadelphia, a Supreme Court Justice issued over five thousand naturalization papers within two weeks to create new voters.

If the North was determined to control votes, the South was even more determined. Nathan Bedford Forrest said in August that five hundred and fifty thousand Southerners belonged to the Klan. He said, "There is not a radical leader in this town [Memphis] but is a marked man, and if trouble should break out, not one of them should be left alive."

Louisiana seemed to be blocked off by terror. Over two thousand people were killed, wounded and otherwise in-jured in Louisiana within a few weeks before the Presiden-tial election. Half the state was overrun by violence—mid-night raids, secret murders, and open riot kept the people in terror. The most remarkable case is that of St. Landry, a planting parish on the river Teche. Here the Republicans had a registered majority of 1,071 votes. In the spring of 1868, they carried the parish by 678. In the fall they gave Grant no votes—not one—while the Democrats cast 4,787, the full vote of the parish. Here occurred one of the blood-iest riots on record, in which the Klan killed and wounded over 200 Republicans, hunting and chasing them for two days and nights through fields and swamps. Thirteen captives were taken from the jail and shot. A pile of twenty-five bodies was found half-buried in the woods. Having conquered the Republicans and driven off the white leaders, the Klan captured the masses, marked them with badges of red flannel, enrolled them in clubs, made them vote the Democratic ticket and then gave them a certificate of the fact.

This was written by Democratic Congressman Samuel S. Cox, of Ohio.

One hundred and twenty corpses were found in the woods or taken out of the Red River after a Negro "hunt" in Bossier parish.

"For ten days prior to the election, the streets of New Orleans were filled with men carrying shot guns, pistols and knives. A band called 'The Innocents' . . . roamed the city hunting for Negroes. Soon no one could be found in the streets. Then the ruffians entered the houses to drive out the blacks, shooting them like rabbits as they ran. A colored man feared to sleep two nights in the same place," wrote E. P. Oberholtzer in his *A History of the United States Since the Civil War*.

"In one month," said General Hatch of the Freedmen's Bureau "two hundred and ninety-seven people were slain in the parishes adjacent to New Orleans."

"The Negroes in Louisiana never recovered from the election murders," General Howard said later. Yet out of this chaos came the first Negro to be elected to the House of Representatives. His name was John W. Menard. He was a slight, attractive man, a college graduate, and his seat was contested by a white Democrat.

Menard had run for the unexpired term in the 40th Congress. His opponent, a General Sheldon, ran for the 41st Congress. Both received the same number of votes, both were declared elected by the same state authority.

When Menard stood up in Washington to present his

credentials the Republicans set off an ovation. But it was his white opponent who was seated, and Menard was convinced the decision was made on the basis of color.

In Georgia, the intimidation took another form. The Democrats had been strong in the convention and were heavily represented in the new legislature. They waited until the state had been readmitted to the Union in June 1868 and congressional protection withdrawn, and then promptly opened a violent attack on the three Negro senators and twenty-nine Negro representatives. They demanded their expulsion. "Their presence was an offense!" They tried every parliamentary device, and finally accused Aaron Bradley of having been arrested on one occasion in New York. Bradley was not allowed to defend himself. He resigned to fight outside the halls.

Bradley was promptly reelected by Savannah Negroes and just as promptly thrown out again.

The Democrats seemed to derive new energy from this success, and outmaneuvered the other two Negro senators, inexperienced men who gained awful knowledge through these weeks.

They were allowed one hour for their joint defense and, after a clamorous debate, were expelled by a vote of 24 to 11. By August, the Democrats turned their full attention on the twenty-nine in the Assembly. Twenty-five of them were ousted. The four who remained were so white in complexion that they could be overlooked. They sat tight. By September, the Democratic organization controlled the legislature and not only declared Negroes ineligible, but began to seat the men who had received the second largest number of votes in the election. The terror in the state was increased.

Henry McNeal Turner, one of the most articulate of the ousted legislators, published the defense speech he had made which had been wiped out of the minutes. The Republicans of Georgia appealed to the State Supreme Court. The Court decided in favor of the expelled legislators, but no one knew how to enforce the ruling. The Negroes petitioned the Governor, Rufus Bullock. He, in turn, petitioned Congress. Congress would not find an answer for many months.

The Radical Republicans were united in supporting Grant for the simple reason that they knew the election of a Democrat would mean the nullification of the Reconstruction Acts. The Democrats had called them "unconstitutional, revolutionary and void." Even Greeley, who disliked Grant with all his heart, said over and over that his defeat would be a national disaster.

Greeley was afflicted with a remarkable optimism. He had arranged in his mind that a half-million immigrants a year from Europe—two-thirds bound for the South—would make a new world with their skills and their ambitions. They—and four years of Grant—would wipe away all the scars of the Civil War.

Grant received a decisive electoral vote, but Seymour carried the popular vote of the South and of important northern states. On November 12, the *Nation* charged that Georgia and Louisiana had been won for Seymour by "organized assassination, and New York and New Jersey by fraud."

When the third session of the 40th Congress met in December 1868, the first business was urgent—a Fifteenth Amendment which would put the right to vote beyond the power of the states.

Johnson went out in a blaze of angry gestures. He announced a general final amnesty for everyone directly or indirectly engaged in the Confederacy. And in his last Presidential message, he suggested that it was the Republicans, with their Reconstruction Acts, who were responsible for the corruption and bloodshed which prevented industrial growth in the South—the only salvation for the Negro.

The Fifteenth Amendment took precedence over everything. Modifications by the opposition were countered by

Republican amendments designed to close up all possible loopholes. At last, on February 26, 1869, before galleries tense and strained, the bill was rollcalled through the House and Senate. With good majorities, it was speeded to the states for ratification.

In the South the new governments had taken power, although Franklin, Louisiana, was "infested by a gang of desperados and thieves," which the civil authorities could not control in any way. The violence was so well organized that ten to one hundred times as many Negroes were killed as whites in the guerrilla warfare that now became a policy.

Negroes who were receiving money wages for building a railroad line between Atlanta and Charlotte, North Carolina were kidnapped and forced back onto plantations where they were brutally beaten if they attempted to escape.

Perhaps the worst aspect of all this was that a new generation was being bred to lawlessness and violence, a generation that was scarcely aware that another way of living was possible.

It was against this carnage that the most remarkable social experiment in American history took its triumphant and tragic way.

☆ 8 ☆

THE DESPISED and the rejected, black and white men and women suddenly discovered that they belonged to the family of man. They discovered that this meant bread and milk, decent clothes, responsibility, and self-government.

It tried every joint and sinew. It shook to the ground the immemorial shibboleth that the power of a master was somehow ordained by God and society.

In this new society, men had the privilege of leaving their ignorance. But the price of this privilege strained the soul. Defending himself on one hand from terror and on the other from ridicule, the black man had to find by some inner grace what it meant to be himself and a friend to others.

The Negro's first impulse was to trust not only his friends but his neighbors. This was not an ingenuous hope. In the days of slavery, fugitives had found help among the slaveless whites. Economic pressures and the bewildering magnificence of a white skin had not completely blinded decent whites to the facts of humanity and common interest.

In all the legislation of these years the Negro saw that his identity and his well-being were based on a common good: the white man was never discriminated against by the Negro legislator. Many white legislators shared this philosophic pragmatism to the bitter end. There were simply not enough of these white men; that was the tragedy.

In the end, it was the Negro who was vilified.

Why? Because he had come so close to success?

Reconstruction was forced to justify itself at a time when war had broken down one society and released the explosive drive of another—when political philosophy was a combination of manifest destiny and the biggest grab.

The ideology of racial inferiority which had hardened the South into a solid whole for a hundred years had been bruised and shaken by the war. But its corruption ran so deep that only a humane ruthlessness would have been strong enough to extirpate it. New fortunes, new aggrandizements on scales unprecedented, did not leave time for such an exercise in moral value.

The fact that the greatest manifestation of democracy in this country collided with the race for markets, reputations, and money is an irony that must be faced. Had cupidity been curbed long enough to allow this democracy to take root, a hundred subsequent years of pain and struggle might very well have been prevented.

The legislatures began to meet in January 1869. "The hell-born policy, which has trampled the fairest and noblest states of our great sisterhood beneath the unholy hoofs of African savages and shoulder-strapped brigands, [giving] the rule to gibbering, louse-eaten, devil-worshipping barbarians from the jungle of Dahomey, and peripatetic buccaneers from Cape Cod Hell, and Boston," was not a very good description of their purpose or of the men who sat in the halls, although it seemed to please the *Fairfield Herald* in South Carolina.

Of course there were greedy and dishonest men among the legislators. Certainly there were stupid and venal men sitting in the assemblies—Negroes who sold their votes and white men who bought them. Of course there were many white Southerners who joined the Negroes for reasons of self-interest, and Negroes who would rather trust the devil than a white man. Certainly there were northern soldiers who stayed in the South to fish a fortune out of the muddied waters.

But these men were few, as the records proved. Too many essentials were at stake.

Negro leaders came, with few exceptions, from two or three groups. From the slave suddenly emancipated, willing and anxious to learn the painful task of self-government; from the fugitive who had been trained in the Abolition movement to an appreciation of his own identity; from the free Negroes, North and South, who were among the first volunteer teachers and Freedmen's agents.

All these men were exposed and reviled the livelong day. They are among the most remarkable and modest men in our history.

The University of South Carolina was now under an interracial board, and Richard Greener of the new generation—first Negro graduate of Havard—would soon be teaching philosophy there. Postmasters in the reconstructed states were, through Grant's new appointments, both white and black; the mail service was better than it had been before the war. Juries, defense and prosecuting lawyers, judges were white and Negro. Justice had a very good name. Balls were given in New Orleans and Charleston, as they had been in the past, but the guests were not limited by color. Courtesy was very much admired, although the mystique of good manners might not be learned overnight.

In South Carolina, Louisiana, and Mississippi were Negro lieutenant governors, men whose reputations survived the worst calumnies. Lynch was Secretary of State in Mississippi. In South Carolina, a Negro with a Pennsylvania law degree sat on the State Supreme Court, and a Negro with a finer education than most white South Carolinians was Superintendent of Schools. The mayor of Natchez, Mississippi, was a Negro. And when the full roster of Congressmen had been run, sixteen Negroes had represented Mississippi, Georgia, North and South Carolina, Alabama, Florida, and Louisiana.

They all served well. Most of them had had a better formal education than Abraham Lincoln.

"The great Negro leader during Reconstruction would have had to have the hardiness of Nkrumah, the ascetic brilliance of Nehru, the adroitness of Franklin D. Roosevelt, and the love-thy-neighbor vocabulary of Martin Luther King, Jr. No such person emerged. No such person, in fact, has ever emerged in America," Lerone Bennett, Jr., writes in *Before the Mayflower*.

Corruption is an easy word to use. As time went on,

and the smoke cleared away, nine-tenths of the charges of corruption in the reconstructed governments were found to be calumnies. The charges were made by the men out of office who wanted in. They were made with the full assumption that any charges against the "uppity-niggers" and the ignorant white would be accepted without question by the unthinking average man.

At the turn of the century, when all trace of the reconstructed governments had vanished and the myth was in full flower, James Garner, a Mississippian and historian, began to compile his study *Reconstruction in Mississippi*. He came to the conclusion that out of a cloaca of charges only two thefts at a state level had taken place: a Negro had stolen books from a public library, a white man had stolen $7,000 from the state. In 1866, before the reconstructed government took office, the state treasurer, a Democrat, had made off with $61,000. Much later, when the Negro legislators were scarcely a memory, another state treasurer took $315,000.

No one will be so color-blind as to believe that a white man is less honest than a Negro. We are merely discussing facts, values, and moral pressures.

What the reconstructed legislatures wished to do, and accomplished, as far as they were able, should be the only standard of evaluation. In every legislature, the same sequence of urgency was followed during this year: civil rights which included ratification of the Fourteenth and Fifteenth Amendments, the establishment of a public school system, revision of taxation, social legislation for the poor and sick, land and labor relations scrutinized, assistance offered to railroads, and other investments.

Every step had to be fought uphill. All the public welfare programs were called irresponsible, wasteful, extravagant, heaped with charges of corruption by those taxpayers who would not benefit from them. Public education came in for endless diatribes, and when the sins of Reconstruction were gathered in the future, the waste of educating Negroes, "making them unfit for work," was examined with a ruthless eye for detail.

These legislators, white and Negro, were concerned with a new deal, a very new one. The responsibility of the state in matters of education had had the barest nod in the past. Even in the North an individual's right to ignorance had a simple sanctity about it.

To the Negro, education and freedom were synonymous. Through their brief period of power, they insisted on maintaining the schools whatever the cost.

"Few people who were not right in the midst of the scenes can form any exact idea of the intense desire which the people of my race showed for education," Booker T. Washington wrote. "As fast as any kind of teachers could be secured, not only were dayschools filled but nightschools as well. A great ambition of the older people was to try to learn to read the Bible before they died . . . Dayschool, nightschool and Sunday School were always crowded, and often many had to be turned away for want of room."

Nonsegregated schooling was stressed by the Negro legislators in all the states. Sometimes this was opposed, sometimes alternatives had to be agreed on, but in most states, the Negroes were able to carry their point. They wanted their children to have the association with white children and profit from the advantages the white children had had. They wanted no divisions. Duplicate schools were also an absurd luxury when the new governments could scarcely meet one set of expenses.

The teachers who came from the North at the end of the war had been so roughly treated that only a few had remained. They had been ostracized and threatened; their schools had been burned. Only those who had been armed with something sturdier than a naïve idealism had been able to survive.

Negro teachers were taking their places as rapidly as possible. In 1869, in South Carolina, there were 8,100 Negro students and 8,200 white. Within a year, there were

16,000 Negro students and almost 12,000 white. The average pay of the teacher was $35 a month. Teachers had to be found; schools had to be built; administrative inexperience overcome, textbooks bought. (In South Carolina textbooks were to be provided at cost or free if a pupil could not afford them.)

Above all, the constant unremitting ridicule had to be met and thrown off.

North Carolina had a very good system, although Florida was not far behind. In Florida, the superintendent was Jonathan Gibbs, a dedicated man, whose own Dartmouth education was better than that of many of his constituents.

In Georgia, the constitution called for a "thorough system of general education to be forever free to all the children of the state," and all the Negro legislators introduced bills on the subject. But the dedicated concern of the other legislators to oust the Negroes deferred all consideration of a public school system until 1870.

In Louisiana, mixed schooling had been on the statute books for some time; but enforcement was another question. The children of the Negro Lieutenant Governor Pinchback were taken to school by a policeman but this did not mean that they would enjoy a full day's schooling. White hoodlums made it a point to disrupt the classes as often as possible.

Through all the clash and fury of these days, the schools somehow survived. They were vilified; the conservatives in the legislatures did all they could to withhold support. Teachers, erratically paid, had to be very devoted to stick it out.

School taxes, more often than not, went into the pockets of the tax collectors, for these funds seemed to offer something irresistibly attractive to venal men. "This . . . was the fault of local county officials," wrote W. E. B. DuBois. "In most cases the leading white landholders, who took no part in the administration of the state, kept their hands upon local taxation and assessments, and were determined that the impoverished propertyholder should not be taxed for Negro education. By various methods, direct and indirect, they continually diverted the school funds, and this class of people were primarily the ones responsible for such dishonesty as there was in the administration of local school funds . . . In North Carolina, $136,000 was collected for education in 1870, but the Department of Education received only $38,931."

And this disposes of one more Reconstruction myth: that the conservative whites were prevented from voting. They voted in every election in every state, and they elected state legislators who, in a number of cases, held the balance of power.

In every southern state the same pattern was followed. The main variations showed in terms of leadership. When the Negroes had gifted leaders and a firm determination to make themselves heard, and strong white allies in the legislatures, good governments were maintained.

Basic principles were basic human needs and desires. This was a recurring political philosophy in each reconstructed state, arrived at independently. There is no evidence of any advice given or taken across state lines; the only possible unifying threads were the Freedmen's agents, but it is probable that agents did no more than assure the Negro that his determination to possess certain rights had an inalienable ring. Even the Republican state parties seemed completely autonomous. Certainly they had little support from Washington.

Sympathetic white legislators were a source of great strength to the Negroes. They were great men, especially the Southerners. For example, R. W. Flourney, the largest slaveowner in Mississippi, threw his heart and soul into the fight for Negro equality.

Why and how such a man gained his convictions is a matter of tireless wonder. Colonel Flourney gave his reasons as deep Christian principles. But most "scalawag" reasons and records were expunged, often by their own families, who in the days of reaction which followed looked upon their activities as skeletons in the closet.

☆ 9 ☆

═══════

LET US briefly take two states, the two which were considered to represent the magnitude and evils of Reconstruction because Negroes were in the majority of the population. These states were South Carolina and Mississippi.

In April 1869, Congress agreed upon a bill which directed that Mississippi be admitted to the Union when the state reconsidered its battered constitution and ratified the Fifteenth Amendment.

Gillam was removed and General Adelbert Ames, acting governor, sent a report to Congress that was a chilling account of murders and outrages. Supported by Congress, Ames began to clean out the civil government and appoint new officeholders. A few Negroes were among the new officials. He also declared freedmen to be competent jurors and made a tentative bid for their political support: "I felt I had a mission to perform in their interests and I unhesitatingly consented to represent them and unite my fortunes with theirs."

In July, Grant ordered the constitution resubmitted, and the Republicans in Mississippi tried again to sew the tattered state together. They favored "an impartial and economic administration of the government, the unrestricted right of speech to all men at all times and places, unrestrained freedom of the ballot, a system of free schools, a reform of the 'iniquitous and unequal' system of taxation and assessments which discriminated against labor." They declared "that all men, without regard to race, color or previous condition of servitude were equal before the law . . ."

General A. L. Alcorn, an aristocratic scalawag who had considered secession treasonable, was nominated for governor, and the Reverend James Lynch, Negro, for secretary of state.

The Klan kept the night and the day clamorous with its protests—Alcorn was venomously attacked as worse than Judas or Benedict Arnold—but those who had the courage to vote ratified the constitution almost unanimously, and Alcorn became the first governor of the reconstructed state.

Mississippi has a particular value as a state from which to draw strong conclusions on Reconstruction. Because of the enormous plantations which had existed like armed kingdoms, Negroes in Mississippi had been so systematically brutalized that Negro leadership was virtually nonexistent in 1865. The speed with which this situation was changed is a phemonenon that is without duplication. Within four years, three congressmen, lieutenant governor, two secretaries of state, a superintendent of education, and a Speaker of the House were all Negroes.

In the first reconstructed legislature (meeting in Jackson on January 11, 1870) were forty Negroes out of one hundred and fifteen members. Republicans were sixty-six; Democrats forty-nine. Almost all were Mississippi-born men, many well-to-do. But ex-slaves represented many of the richest plantation counties.

The legislature immediately ratified the Fourteenth and Fifteenth Amendments. Mississippi was formally received back into the Union, although it took two weeks of debate to overcome the deep apprehensions of the Republicans.

And two senators started off for Washington: General Ames and Hiram Revels.

Poetic justice has never been so well served. In 1861, Jefferson Davis had left Washington in the middle of his term as senator to become President of the Confederacy. In 1870, Hiram Revels, in his frock coat, stepped onto the railway cars for Washington to fill out Davis' term. Hiram Revels was a Negro.

Revels had been born in North Carolina and escaped to Indiana where he had gotten an education. After graduating from Knox College in Illinois, he came to Baltimore as a minister in 1860. There he helped to organize two colored regiments. For two years he taught school in St. Louis, then the Freedmen's Bureau engaged him as an agent, and thus he found his way to Mississippi. There was very little about the dark side of Negro life he did not know. He was a man of imposing appearance, forty-eight years old at this time, with the sharp intelligence that is often the attribute of a self-made man. Apparently he had few political ambitions, for he seemed genuinely surprised when elected to Jefferson Davis' seat.

He arrived in Washington in February 1870, and presented his credentials. The credentials had been signed by Brevet Major General and Provisional Governor of Mississippi Ames. (General Ames had signed his own credentials as well.)

It was a point of great nicety which, considering the daily need for inspired improvisation, could have been acknowledged by Congress with a bow. But Senator Saulsbury of Delaware chose to make it a point of grave issue. For three days the Senate debated the propriety of accepting Revels' credentials.

James G. Blaine, Speaker of the House, wrote later on, "His presence while demonstrating the extent to which the assertion of equal rights had been carried, served to increase and stimulate the Southern resistance to the whole system of Republican reconstruction."

Revels was not a man one could argue away. He was better educated than many who sat in Congress; he was experienced; he was competent; he was elected. He sat out the embarrassment of Congress with great composure. Sumner made a powerful speech in his support, and brought the foolish comedy to an end. Revels introduced himself in a speech which testified to a civilized man.

"Mr. President, I maintain that the past record of my race is a true index of the feelings which today animate them. They bear toward their former masters no revengeful thoughts, no hatred, no animosity. They aim not to elevate themselves by sacrificing one single interest of their fellow white citizens. They ask but the rights which are theirs by God's natural law and which are the natural growth, the logical sequence of the conditions in which the legislative enactments of this nation have placed them. They appeal to you and to me to see that they receive that protection which alone will enable them to pursue their daily vocations with success and enjoy the liberties of citizenship on the same footing with their white neighbors and friends."

General Ames, having signed his own credentials, had an even more difficult time. It took several weeks of lofty oratory and quick sharp retorts to get him admitted.

The new administration in Jackson had to start from the bottom. The credit of the state had virtually come to an end. Borrowed money carried a high rate of interest. The assessable valuation of taxable property was very low, and yet taxes had to be imposed at a high rate.

A whole new code of laws had to be discussed and drawn up, for the Black Codes which had ruled the state were repealed the moment the new government took power. The legislature agreed that its "true intent and meaning" was to wipe out all laws "which in any manner recognized any natural difference or distinction between citizens and inhabitants of the state."

A new judiciary was needed, thirty-eight judges in all.

This in itself was an appalling problem, for there were few men who combined legal training with social enlightenment. Yet the men who became judges were never charged with political corruption.

A completely new school system had to be started without delay. In the entire state there was only a handful of school buildings, and those in melancholy need of repair. This meant an enormous expenditure of cash, and the struggle of inexperienced men to find the money was a painful lesson in self-government.

Day after day, the legislature worked to learn the basic rules by which a community of human beings must live and flourish. New Republican legislators, many of whom did not have two pairs of overalls to their names, refused to yield a point until every possible confusion of interpretation had been erased.

It took six months. Three hundred and twenty-five acts and resolutions were passed. Some of them may have been redundant, but the desire of the legislators was to leave nothing to chance. Protection of civil rights took up many of the resolutions, for, as Governor Alcorn said, "all citizens should be shielded by the law as with a panoply."

Years later the Republicans were blamed for "oppressions, robberies and dishonesty as proved by the fearful rate of taxation." No one seemed to have a clear notion of the percent of taxes on the dollar. It had been "awful," "fearful," "monstrous," but it was actually a little less than nine mills on the dollar of which almost one-fifth was for public schools. A Mississippi "scalawag" said later, "This was the true answer, but every Klansman knew better than to answer the question, for one of the founders of that order wrote confidently to an associate that they must appeal to the world 'as a wretched, downtrodden and impoverished people.'"

The impasse in Mississippi turned finally on the economics of "color." The bulk of the Negroes were laborers; they were not artisans or property owners. If the poor whites, who were also without skills or property, had joined politically with the Negroes they would have dominated the property owners. But they were whites: the color of their skin was about all they had to sell and the offering price was high.

This period still remained the height of hope. No one wished to be responsible for magnifying the serpents in this garden of the newborn. Yet men were not fools. The poor men, especially, knew how exposed they were.

The Freedmen's Bureau received no further congressional support after 1869, although it continued to offer what help it could until 1874. In the three years between 1867 and 1870, it had appropriated $3,521,934 for schools. (Churches and mission societies had spent $1,572,287 for this same period, and the freedmen themselves had given, in cash, for the schools $785,700.)

With only a thin line of Union soldiers remaining in the state, the defense of schools and voters fell to the Negro militia of the Union Leagues.

In South Carolina the Negro militias also played a large part.

South Carolina differed from Mississippi in the degree of education of its legislators. The first governor of the reconstructed state was a Pennsylvanian named Robert K. Scott. He had been a colonel in the Union army, an assistant commissioner of the Freedmen's Bureau. He was a man of infinite goodwill but he lacked the forcefulness and acumen that were indispensable to this social revolution. His difficulties confound the imagination.

Negro legislators were in the majority but never in control.

The Washington correspondent of the *New York Tribune,* a conservative named James Pike, went to see with his own eyes a South Carolina legislative session. He came away fuzzily convinced that he had seen something more remarkable than he fully understood.

"About three-fourths of the crowd belonged to the African race. They were of every hue, from the octoroon to the deep black. They were such a looking body of men as might pour out of a market house or a court house at random in any southern state. . . . Their dress was as varied as their countenances. There was the second-hand frock coat of infirm gentility, glossy and threadbare. There was the stovepipe hat of many ironings and departed styles. There was also to be seen a total disregard of the proprieties of costume in the coarse and dirty garments of the field. In some instances rough woolen comforters embraced the neck and hid the absence of linen. Heavy brogans and short torn trousers, it was impossible to hide.

"The Speaker is black, the Clerk is black, the doorkeepers are black, the little pages are black, the chairman of the Ways and Means is black, and the chaplain is coal black. At some of the desks sit colored men whose types it would be hard to find outside of the Congo.

"The leading topics of discussion are all well understood by the members, as they are of a practical character and appeal directly to the personal interests of every legislator as well as those of his constituents. When an appropriation bill is up to raise money to catch and punish the KKK, they know exactly what it means. . . . So too with educational measures. The free school comes right home to them; then the business of arming and drilling the militia.

"The laughing propensity of the sable crowd is a great cause of disorder. . . . But beneath all this shocking burlesque upon legislative proceedings, we must not forget that there is something real to this uncouth and untutored multitude . . . They have a genuine interest and a genuine earnestness in the business of the assembly which we are bound to recognize and respect. . . . They have an earnest purpose borne of a conviction that their position and their condition are not fully assured which lends a sort of dignity to their proceedings."

The common school system was organized temporarily at the first session and permanently in 1870. Poor men were given relief in the form of money or supplies, and a land commissioner was appointed, under a board, to buy land for cheap resale to landless farmers. An orphan asylum was authorized, and an institution for the deaf, dumb, and blind was established: it functioned until 1873, when the white faculty resigned because they did not wish to train Negro students for the work. An insane asylum was set up and Negro patients admitted.

High taxation was again the most serious problem. Men who had never had money in their pockets were called on to disburse large sums. Taxes were the only way to raise those sums and the purposes were imperative.

Before the war, South Carolina taxation had spared the planter with slaves and put the burden on the merchants, bankers, and storekeepers. These professional men had paid five or six times as much as the planters. The state now tried to put a uniform taxation on all property at its full value. The rate was increased to pay for the schools, asylums, and poor-care.

Many refused to pay taxes—or could not pay. Many tax collectors pocketed what they took.

Railroad speculation struck South Carolina. Railroads were the new golden path to everywhere. Every state must have its railroads no matter what the cost. Without them neither money nor goods nor industrial life would have moved. State subsidies were given with an element of hysteria.

In South Carolina, as in all the other southern states, very little money had been spent since the end of the war. Roads and public buildings and bridges were in terrible disrepair. Money was spent as though it came from an endless fount. The metaphysics of all this is fascinating; it is hard to know what attitude but a metaphysical one would have been appropriate. Northern banks would not lend money "because of lawless bands." The assumption of loaves-and-fishes was perhaps merely a pragmatic attitude which did not quite come off.

In South Carolina the first split in the Republican party took place. Few wished to regard it as crucial, for it was essential to believe that there would be plenty of time to get the future squarely on its feet. Meanwhile, the second Negro congressman to have his credentials accepted arrived in Washington in the fall of 1870. Joseph T. Rainey was an elegant, fair-skinned man with mutton-chop whiskers. He had been born of parents who had bought their own freedom, and had had no education except the lessons he could teach himself. When he reached Washington, he began to call for federal aid to education. He was the first American to do so.

By the end of 1870, the activities of terrorists were so widespread that Grant, in a special message to Congress, said that "the free exercise of franchise has by violence and intimidation been denied to citizens in several of the states lately in rebellion."

Yet he took no action when the governor of North Carolina sent urgent pleas for federal troops to lift the siege of two counties completely dominated by the Klan. When South Carolina asked for assistance in March 1871, he ordered the Klan to disperse within thirty days, and he sent a special message to Congress asking for legislation which would give him power to act.

The House responded with alacrity, almost as though it were a war measure, but the Senate split dangerously on the request. However, a bill was finally passed which gave the President power to move. Called the Ku Klux Act, it allowed him to suspend the writ of habeas corpus when lawlessness constituted "rebellion against the United States," and to establish martial law.

There were less than nine thousand soldiers in the South. Grant hesitated to use his new power too freely, since words without deeds would have been disastrous. Indeed, he used it only in the case of South Carolina, when troops took over control of nine counties in South Carolina and arrested nearly six hundred people.

This induced horror in the Democrats, and even conservative Republicans, who had remained silent when evidence of outrages against Negroes were offered, protested the arrest of white men.

But the evidence was incontrovertible. Even more alarming than the terror was the fact that, though six hundred and forty people had been indicted for murders and outrages in the federal courts of Mississippi, only two hundred were arrested and not a single one convicted.

By the spring of 1871, the evidence before Congress had piled as high as a levee—evidence of juries refusing to return verdicts, even when names, dates, and places were specified; of witnesses too frightened to testify; of registration prevented by every ruse and tactic of the human mind. Congress authorized a Joint Committee of twenty-one members to make intensive inquiries. Three subcommittees set out for the South to take testimony.

This was probably one of the most exhaustive congressional inquiries ever made, although many witnesses were extremely evasive. General Forrest, when pressed, let loose a stream of invectives and insisted there was no such thing as the Klan.

As a matter of fact, it had gone underground in 1869, and was functioning through many splinter groups. Most of the former Confederates said the trouble was all in the imagination and flatly denied the existence of armed groups. The Negroes told a different story. They made "good witnesses and told graphic and convincing stories which had the ring of truth."

It was the last effort made by Congress to win the Civil War.

Sumner, like a weary machine, was offering his Civil Rights Bill in almost every form he could conceive. He used all the parliamentary devices of which he was a master, for he did not think there was very much time.

The Republicans felt they must maintain political hegemony but not at the price of continuous upheaval. A complex reasoning began with the thought that the Negro was somehow at fault and should quiet down. Negro congressmen attempted to answer these charges. Robert DeLarge, who was now in Congress from South Carolina, made a slashing speech, as did Rainey. But the Radical Republicans hda acquired some strange bedfellows, and they were beginning to stir uneasily in their sleep.

A whole new middle class was developing with the new industries of the South. Textile mills were spreading through the Carolinas; cotton factories were opening in Georgia; tobacco was becoming a southern industry; iron and coal were promising vast fortunes in Virginia, Tennessee, Alabama. They all represented a combination of northern money and southern labor, and unrest would be fatal to their continued harmony.

The Negroes had no place to go but the Republican party, which they were beginning to embarrass. The Negroe's loyalty was unshaken, but they had to face the bitter fact that their party's loyalty was not as fixed as the stars. The fatal split in the party of Lincoln had begun and would spread through the nation.

☆ I O ☆

BY 1 8 7 1, almost all the South Carolina Negro legislators knew how to read and write. Many of them were forceful and eloquent speakers. This gave them the confidence to venture on an independent course.

R. H. King, a member of the legislature, started a Negro reform movement which would insure that "honest mechanics and farmers whose minds are not biased . . . who are identified with prosperity and the people's interest" would be elected to the state government.

Robert DeLarge, Beverly Nash and Robert Smalls, all very strong men in the government, tried to form a new political party, for the soaring state debt disturbed them and they wished to have a free hand with the financial problems of the state.

They were also deeply uneasy over the confusions in the national Republican party. The scandals of the Grant administration did not help the charges of corruption in South Carolina. They listened to old friends in Washington who were equally distressed by the signs of split among the Republicans and hoped that the Negroes would choose the winning side.

But Elliott and Cardozo opposed any divisive action. They felt that, weak and torn as the Republicans were in South Carolina, the only chance of economic progress and a secure vote lay with the national party. They did not trust the combinations that would have to be made if a new party were organized. It was a choice of lesser evils.

A third Negro congressman was sent from South Carolina to Washington that year. Alonzo J. Ransier, the man who had remarked that "in proportion to the education of the people, so is their progress in civilization," had just served a term as lieutenant governor. He made a speech in Charleston and spoke for Negro Republicans. "I am no apologist for thieves . . . I am in favor of a more thorough investigation of the official conduct of any and every public official if there is anything like well-grounded suspicion . . . [However] such is the determined opposition to the Republican party by our opponents that no administration of our affairs, however honest, just and economical, would satisfy any considerable portion of the Democratic masses

. . . Let each man act as if, by his individual vote, he could wipe out the odium resting upon our party and help to remove the evils that afflict us at present. Let him feel, black or white, that the country holds him responsible for the shortcomings of his party and that it demands of him the elevation to public position of men who are above suspicion. Let each man feel that he is responsible for every dollar of public money, for every schoolhouse closed against his children . . . [Thus] the community as a whole is protected and the equal rights of all guaranteed and made safe."

By 1871, in spite of the commotion and upheavals, nearly two thousand small farms had been occupied—or would be soon occupied—by landless farmers who would have eight years in which to make payment.

South Carolina had been completely dominated (it was said) by one hundred and eighty great landlords. On their plantations most of the government had been carried on. To break this power, as the new constitution did, was to create a social change so profound as to explore the very essence of government.

"Both the poor whites and the Negroes were not only poverty-stricken, but, for that reason, peculiarly susceptible to petty graft and bribery. Economically they had always been stripped bare; a little cash was a curiosity and a few dollars a fortune," W. E. B. DuBois writes in *Black Reconstruction*. "The sale of their votes and political influence was from the first, simply a matter of their knowledge and conception, of what the vote was for and what it could procure. With experience their conception of its value rose until some of them conceived the idea of making the ballot a power by which they could change their social and economic status and live like human beings. . . . When one considers that this was a day when the line between using political power for personal advantage and using it for social uplift was dim and difficult to follow throughout the whole nation, the wonder is that the labor

139

vote of South Carolina so easily ranged itself behind the new school system, the orphanages, the land distribution and the movements toward reform in public efficiency."

When taxes failed to raise the necessary revenue, the state appealed to northern banks. Loans were negotiated at rates of interest running from 15 to 20 percent; with additional commissions to financial agents, $3,200,000 cost the state $9,514,000 in bonds.

Administrative power was held, all through this period, by the white legislators.

A white Southerner named C. W. Dudley said, rather wistfully one imagines, "The colored population must give us their assistance in any reforms which are contemplated. If they have turned from us—from a suspicion that their newly acquired rights had been grudgingly granted and were not safe in the hands of those who had never recognized them as equals—this was but natural; and we are compelled to admit that under similar circumstances we would have done so ourselves."

Louisiana Republican leaders were less interested in reform than survival. They even turned their eyes toward the thick and protecting walls of the Democratic party.

If the opprobrious use of "scalawag" and "carpetbagger" ever had a valid meaning, it was in Louisiana. The battle of Louisiana was the most dramatic and unpredictable of all those in the reconstructed states because of the state's unique social structure. In New Orleans, Negroes and whites had mingled for so long that many Negroes could pass as whites, both physically as well as temperamentally. They had little feeling for the country slaves, black as night, who had had no education till freedom dawned. The great mass of black and white poor folk were often quite forgotten in the intricate maneuvering of power in New Orleans.

The Republicans had finally won the loyalty of the Negroes, but the party was so shaken with graft that a group of legislators led by Oscar Dunn, the former slave and now lieutenant governor, attempted a revolt within the state convention of 1870.

The governor was Henry Clay Warmoth, that gay and unscrupulous young man who claimed he had not a drop of northern blood. Although he was a Republican, his best friends were the planters and he had succeeded in establishing a machine that worked faultlessly for H. C. Warmoth.

By candid trickery, he gained control of the election apparatus, and was able to throw out votes on any pretext whatever. He survived the revolt led by Dunn by enlisting the full support of the planters. But when the legislature met in 1871, he found that the Negroes were almost to a man against him. By summer, the state party had divided, Dunn heading one faction, Warmoth the other—and this reflected the graver, wider division in the North.

In the fall of 1871, Sumner made a last desperate effort to get a Civil Rights Bill passed. His bill was aimed at the North as well as the South. He wished protection from discrimination in railroads, theaters, hotels, schools, cemeteries, churches—and in the jury box. On Sumner rested nearly the whole burden of defending the dream of equal rights. Even senators like Schurz were becoming moderates.

He presented petitions he had gathered for the bill; he tried parliamentary ruses, he attempted to make the holiday adjournment conditional on a vote. At last, he seized on a desperate but striking gamble.

An amnesty bill dealing with the last odds and ends of land titles had passed the House. Sumner moved that the Civil Rights Bill should be an amendment to it.

An act of justice and an act of generosity linked together; he believed that such a bill would pass by a two-thirds vote. Amnesty and Civil Rights were lost by a single vote, and he promptly offered the bill again.

"I entreat Senators over the way [Democrats] who really seek reconciliation now to unite in this honest effort.

Give me an opportunity to vote for this bill. I long to do it. Gladly would I reach out the olive branch; but I know no way that can be done unless you begin by justice to the colored race."

During the Christmas holidays, Negroes held mass meetings, agitated, petitioned. When the recess was over, they filled the galleries whenever Sumner was scheduled to speak. He read letters, newspapers, documents to prove the necessity of the bill. His Negro friends supplied him with the sweepings of wastebaskets to prove his point.

Charles Sumner had fought a long fight. It reached over twenty-five years. He had never weakened his conviction that this fight must be won. His voice grew hoarse with his fears that this last hope would be taken from him.

"I appeal for the sake of peace, so that at last there shall be an end to slavery, and the rights of the citizens shall be everywhere under the equal safeguard of the national law . . . Humbly do I pray that the Republic may not lose this great prize, or postpone its enjoyment."

But Sumner's party was closing the doors on one of its great men. The new generation of Republicans could not afford such a man, according to the banking and railroad Cookes. "You know how I have felt for a long time in regard to . . . the ultra-infidelic radicals like Sumner, Ben Wade, Stevens," Henry Cooke wrote to a friend. "They were dragging the Republican party into all sorts of isms and extremes. . . . These reckless demagogues have had their day and the time has come for wiser counsel."

These "demagogues" had consistently fought the railroads in behalf of the farmers whose land was being confiscated; they had been on the side of labor and the nascent unions; Sumner, as chairman of the Foreign Relations Committee, had consistently held to broader views than a clamorously self-confident "nationalism" had found congenial.

The handful of Republicans who still believed in the

abolition-democracy ideals were unable to give up the dream of a peaceful revolution—a social change with the Negro free and endowed, the result of a merciful agreement by all, but they were growing old and the fire had left them.

Sumner's "interminable" efforts at a Civil Rights Bill made him a great bore to his restless, let's-get-on-with-business colleagues. Brisk up-and-coming men found his moral arguments tiresome liabilities.

Many of these new Republicans reflected a "sober, thoughtful middle class, equally removed from wealth and poverty," as *The Nation* said. They stood midway: the fathers had ties with the past, the sons had intimations of the future; both wanted moral rectitude but at the same time no interference with sound investments and enterprising business deals. In the past the fathers had provided bulk for the antislavery movement and yet had held a high and conservative appreciation of property. If a man could not feel safe with what belonged to him, what security could society have? Yet the older generation had managed to square this empiric question with a lofty moral sense which had led them to denounce men's investment and holdings in human flesh. They had given to their sons a deep, genuine horror at race enslavement, yet both fathers and sons felt a profound distress at any hint of land confiscation and great uneasiness at any appearance of federal interference with the states. States' rights had the clarion ring of 1776. The Freedmen's Bureau, the army occupation, even the Fourteenth and Fifteenth Amendments had left them uneasily searching the consciences of the Founding Fathers.

More ramified southern investments might be an answer. Honest, morally clean northern money invested to stabilize a situation to everyone's advantage—this had an element of divine inspiration. But investments with such high promise required stability at any price. "Where economic interests jibed," a modern historian, Paul H. Buck, has written, "men of business were men of peace."

It had been officially reported in 1869 that "within five years more cotton spindles have been put in motion, more iron furnaces erected, more iron smelted, more bars rolled, more steel made, more coal and copper mined, more lumber sawn and hewn, more houses and shops constructed, more manufactories of different kinds started and more petroleum collected, refined and exported than during any equal period in the history of the country."

Here indeed lay law and order, security of salaries and investments, lower rates on railroads, increased land values. Everyone, Negro and white, desired this perfect republic.

This "sober thoughtful middle class" became convinced that this was the ideal way of protecting the Negro. . . . Peace, prosperity, should be coupled with a confidence in the innate goodness of those men whose homeland was the South, who knew the Negroes as well as their own children.

Let forgiveness reign? Let those men of probity restrain the small lawless bands of ruffians called the Klan?

These soul-questions were made easier because they were laced through with deep embarrassment. The Grant administration was topheavy with charges of graft, corruption, and fraud. If the Democrats could also prove their charges of graft, corruption and fraud in the Republican governments of the South, the burden for honest and honorable middle class northern Republicans would become almost intolerable.

The Republican party of Missouri had split on tactics in 1870, and the "liberal" Republicans had by 1872 gained such strength that they were able to plan their own convention.

The disquieting picture of a threefold Republican party now faced the friends of the Negro. The conservatives were grouped around Grant, the "liberals" grouped around men like Carl Schurz and Rutherford B. Hayes, and the remnant of the Radical Republicans shook their tattered banners with Sumner.

Sumner had been dismayed when the break became wide enough for a separate convention. He refused to go with the bolters. Since he had already broken with Grant, he was obviously expendable to both sides.

Many hoped that the "liberals" would so dominate the party itself that a split would not be permanent. But others, like Schurz, believed a new party was essential.

The convention called in Cincinnati the spring of 1872 was rich in leaders; it had the support of several powerful newspapers. Sumner was not needed.

Their choice for President—after three or four tries—was Horace Greeley. As editor and reformer, he had played a strong part in western development—"Go West, young man!"—and now he was saying, "Go South, industry and capital!" Years before, Andrew Johnson had said of Greeley that he had "so much goodness of heart as to produce infirmity of mind . . ." He was "a sublime old child."

Greeley now begged for a "national reconstruction" —hands clasped across the chasm "in the joyous consciousness that [old enemies] are and must henceforth remain bretheren."

The liberal Republican platform called for the removal of any last disqualifications for white voters, the end of military rule and federal control, suffrage and equal rights for Negroes.

"We are a party of fools," Greeley had once told Sumner with perfect foresight.

Just before the Cincinnati convention closed, the Amnesty Act was passed by Congress without the Civil Rights amendment. True, one could not keep a remnant of citizens off-balance forever. Sumner had merely suggested that there should be a counterbalance until the Negro's position was secured. Sumner spoke with a bitter sadness,

"You must be just to the colored man before you are generous to former rebels."

The Cincinnati convention caused a fatal cleavage in the Republican parties of South Carolina and Louisiana.

Warmoth headed the Louisiana delegation to Cincinnati. The convention had materialized at precisely the right moment to save his skin. He had been so clever and unscrupulous that an investigating committee from Washington had arrived to see what could be done about such a man. He promptly gathered together one hundred and twenty-five delegates—the largest contingent at Cincinnati —and arrived in Ohio with his pockets bulging with proof that the enemies of true reform were in the Grant faction.

His reputation was not unknown to the Republican "liberals"—they did not really want his kind at all—but his good-natured frankness was very disarming. That an archgrafter should ally himself with this convention opposed to graft had a revivalist ring about it. And he also assured electoral votes.

At home, meanwhile, Oscar Dunn was acting governor. He took the opportunity to bid for "the aid and cooperation of every colored man in the state. An effort is being made to sell us out to the Democrats by the governor and we must nip it in the bud . . . We want for ourselves and the people of all parties better laws on the statute books and better men to administer them, and we are persuaded that neither of these wants will ever be met so long as the present executive exercises any material control over the politics of Louisiana . . . The people are gravely and earnestly fighting for their personal and political rights."

The Congressional Committee solemnly read Warmoth out of the party. Impeachment loomed. But when Warmoth returned from Cincinnati, he handled the situation briskly. He joined with the Democrats, as Dunn had foretold, and canceled all that Dunn as acting governor had set in motion. Within a few months, Dunn was dead—

some claimed by foul play, though without real evidence.

South Carolina had also sent a delegation to Cincinnati, headed by D. H. Chamberlain who would, in another two years, be governor. Chamberlain, a white Northerner, carried with him a program of reform. The delegation was small. It lacked the support of the more astute Negro legislators, who were deeply afraid of any division within the party. The justification of their fears blossomed like a man-eating plant in July.

When the conservative Republicans met in Philadelphia, in early June, they were like rollicking colts. They seemed utterly unperturbed by charges of thieves caught red-handed, or by the Cincinnati convention.

In July, the Democrats met, *endorsed the entire Cincinnati platform of the Liberal Republicans*, and chose as their nominee—Horace Greeley.

The Presidential campaign was one of the strangest in our history. It teetered between ambivalences and equivocations. The Liberal Republicans tried to behave as though a grinning Democratic monkey was not riding on their shoulders wherever they went. The Grant Republicans were beset by both calumnies and truths about Grant and his large family. In those days no holds were barred. Grant bore himself in a close-lipped careful way and let others do the talking.

Sumner had attacked him in a massive speech in the Senate before packed galleries. On the street, people stopped each other to say, "Sumner is attacking Grant." It generated a feeling like physical assault.

Sumner's charges were almost wholly of nepotism, of faulty use of troops at elections, of a man not to be trusted in his high office. The speech detailed its charges so fully that it became the book and precept of the Greeley Republicans.

It was also used line by line to *defend* the "man of Appomattox."

147

Horace Greeley found himself in the dream-like position of being the chosen vessel of dissident Republicans and Democrats. He had spent his adult life as a reformer, but was a man with whom the Abolitionists had never felt a real ease. Probably the "liberal" Republicans were inspired when they selected him, for who else would have embodied the wobbly ingenuous philosophy they had put forth?

He gave streams of advice to the Negro through the *New York Tribune:* Be realistic. Political equality is far off. Social equality will remain forever out of reach. Don't expect free gifts of land. Face things as they are. Segregate yourselves; employ each other. Who are your best friends? *Sound, conservative, knowing, white Southerners.*

Why, he was a true Democrat! He succeeded in simplifying almost every problem. Universal amnesty, impartial suffrage were all that were needed to bring southern whites and Negroes together at a perpetual barbecue. The blood, the violence at the polls were the work of irresponsible boys or bona fide criminals.

The joint congressional report on the Klan appeared that spring. The work was exhaustive and filled thirteen volumes. It had all the possibilities of a remarkable campaign document, but it was largely ignored.

The Democratic members of the committee made a minority report showing their dislike for the whole business. They blamed corruption and terror on the Republicans. The Republican members recommended protective measures until all federal laws were obeyed.

The report showed that questions had been asked high and low. The section on South Carolina was a "mass of revolting details." "Elias Hill was a colored man who had from infancy been dwarfed in legs and arms. He was unable to use either. But he was highly respected . . . It was on this ground that he was visited by the Ku Klux Klan, brutally beaten and dragged from his house into the yard where he was left in the cold at night, unable to walk or crawl."

Ninety-seven Negroes were reported killed and one hundred and forty-six wounded or whipped. Negro churches were burned. Colored women beaten and raped; men maimed and castrated. Negro artisans were the special objects of attack.

Negroes did not look for trouble, but they defended themselves. Occasional whites protected Negroes from other whites at great danger to themselves. "In the nine [South Carolina] counties covered by the investigation, for the period of approximately six months," the report continued, "the KKK lynched and murdered thirty-five men, whipped two hundred and sixty-two men and women, otherwise outraged, shot, multilated, burned out, etc., one hundred and one persons. It committed cases of sex offenses against Negro women. During this time, the Negroes killed four men, beat one man, committed sixteen other outrages, but no case of torture. No case is found of a white woman seduced or raped by a Negro."

In Mississippi, a state senator, Charles Caldwell, had been killed in broad daylight by a fusillade so massive that he was "grotesquely turned completely over by the impact of the innumerable shots at close range."

The majority of white Southerners questioned denied all knowledge of the Klan.

Everyone agreed that the Enforcement Act against the Klan could not be enforced even in a token away.

Its legal life expired during the campaign. It was quietly interred.

Grant's election may well have been a personal triumph.

Greeley carried only six states. In the North, the Democrats stayed away from the polls in spectacular numbers.

Before the electoral vote was counted, Greeley died,

adding the last ironic touch to a situation compounded of improbabilities.

The Democrats won in Maryland, Kentucky, Missouri, Tennessee, Georgia, and Texas, where any connection with Greeley Republicans was quietly forgotten.

Georgia returned to the rule of the planters after two years of a Democratic legislature.

The shadows of more ominous events began to lengthen.

☆ I I ☆

═══════

THE NEGROES felt a shock as sudden as an earthquake. Their struggle within the southern governments for adequate representation had been a basic issue, not a fight for spoils. They trusted no one to enforce their rights but themselves. When the gulf between Republicans began to widen through the states, the Negro was at first bewildered, then convinced that he had better have a foot in both camps. The Negroes' fear which always lay close to the surface put the blame for this new trouble on planters, carpetbaggers, scalawags—anyone with a white skin, for anyone with a white skin was eligible for membership in the Klan.

If national politics were virtually impossible to disentangle in this campaign, how can we begin to unwind Louisiana?

The Klan Democrats were represented in the state elections by an archly anti-Negro Confederate general named John McEnery. He was a planter from a parish in which more Negro and white Republicans had been killed than in any other.

Confederate General P. G. T. Beauregard had headed a Reform party with a platform, "Justice to all races, creeds and political opinions, and full equality in all public places, vehicles and schools."

The Greeley Republicans nominated D. B. Penn and a Negro, Francis Dumas.

The Grant Republicans had nominated W. P. Kellogg, a Union man who had settled in Louisiana, and gave him a Negro running-mate, C. C. Antoine.

Warmoth, who lacked only honesty and integrity to be a great reformer, had tried his best to bring together Greeley's Penn and the Democrats' McEnery in a new coalition with a Negro as Secretary of State, and Pinchback as congressman-at-large.

But General McEnery declined the honor and so Warmoth deserted his old colleagues and joined McEnery. Pinchback decided the least crooked path back to reform lay with the regular Republicans.

There is little question that Beauregard's party had a remarkable platform of complete equality right down the line. But distrust of white men and their parties ran so deep that Kellogg and the familiar Republicans were voted in.

Pinchback, who had succeeded Dunn as lieutenant governor, remained the strong leader among the Negroes. Where Oscar Dunn had been incorruptible, Pinchback was far more guileful.

Warmoth was quick to salvage what he could. He sought to set up a rival Returning Board to count the election results. The fraud, intimidation, and violence of the campaign might make this a reasonable though illegal gesture from any man but Warmoth. His action merely intensified fraud, intimidation, and violence, and for two months, two governors ruled in Louisiana.

It was the responsibility of Congress to put an end to such a situation. Grant pleaded for decisive action, which meant support of Kellogg who had legally won the election. But Warmoth was holding on to the chair, keeping it warm, presumably for McEnery. Grant was most reluctant to send in additional troops but when Congress declined responsibility, he was forced to move.

In mid-December, Warmoth was impeached and for forty-three intense and crucial days, Louisiana had a Negro governor, Pinchback. Open warfare blazed. Negroes were murdered without a chance to protect themselves, for efforts to arm them legally met shocked opposition, even in the North.

With the decision of the Returning Board, Pinchback stepped down and Kellogg stepped up, but McEnery's supporters fought the troops. Kellogg was driven out of the state house. Soldiers reinstalled him.

On March 4, 1873, Grant made his inaugural address. Peace had at last come, he said, throughout the country.

At the very moment he was talking, Kellogg had been ousted once more and fighting had broken out in the streets of New Orleans.

Kellogg was pushed in the door a third time, and this time he was able to stay.

But it did not mean peace. On Easter Sunday, Negroes barricaded themselves in the courthouses at Colfax and were literally cannonaded out by the white militia. As they fled, the artillery mowed down sixty-one Negroes and thirty-seven were shot in cold blood after they had surrendered. Grant called it "a butchery of citizens which in bloodthirstiness and barbarity is hardly surpassed by any acts of savage warfare." Insuperable obstacles were thrown in the way of punishing these murderers, and the so-called conservative papers of the state not only justified the massacre but denounced as federal tyranny the attempt of the United States officers to bring them to justice.

While Louisiana was undergoing her punishment, Alabama was facing Klan action of almost incredible ruthlessness. A Republican had been elected governor, but the Democrats seized the state house and claimed to have won the election. The Republicans settled down in the United States Court House.

In Alabama, white solidarity had seemed so important to the Democrats that the Klan had acted with more brutality against the poor whites than against the Negroes. Northern capital had in its ingenuous way supported the mischief by pouring money into the coal and iron sections of the state where the poor whites predominated. (Birmingham had been incorporated in 1871.)

Once more, an appeal went to Congress. Once more, Grant had to intervene. In December, he submitted an unofficial compromise, and the Republicans were able to hold on to the governorship.

In Arkansas, the Republican split resulted in two governments. In Austin and Helena, Arkansas, armed Negroes, supporting Grant, fought all attempts by the Democrats to oust their elected officials. In Little Rock, pitched battles tore up the streets. One side held the state house, the other, the railroad and the telegraph office. This situation lasted until 1874, when the Republicans were confirmed.

In Texas, the Klan had succeeded in keeping the Negroes from the polls. The Democrats won the legislature and elected all the congressmen. The Union League militia, however, supported the Republicans who refused to surrender the State House. This time Grant refused to send in troops and the Republicans were obliged to yield to the Democrats.

The "liberal" Republican convention had greatly alarmed the Negroes of Mississippi. They did not wait for instructions, but gave their support to Governor Ames and

153

the Grant ticket. Mississippi Negroes had developed in remarkable ways, against almost insuperable odds. They served on juries, and this meant, in Mississippi, a function similar to that of a county commissioner in the North. Planters complained bitterly that "nine out of ten who sit on the juries are ignorant, without property, and yet are permitted to judge what is best for the interest of property holders."

In the heart of the Black Belt, the sheriff, the majority of the magistrates, and all county officials, except one, were now Negroes.

About this time the *Jackson Clarion,* the Democratic party organ in the state, made an unusual statement: "While they [the Negroes] have been naturally tenacious of their newly acquired privileges, their general conduct will bear them witness that they have shown consideration for the feelings of the whites. . . . The only color line which has existed grew out of the unwise policy which had previously been pursued by the Democratic party in its efforts to prevent the enjoyment by the newly emancipated race of the rights and privileges to which they are entitled."

The average colored legislator was suspicious, eager, wary, and highly defensive for good reasons. The Negroes cherished their reputations for honesty; their efforts to learn were constant and intense. The jealousies among the Republicans alarmed them deeply for they saw only themselves as the losers.

The Greeley Republicans has roused their apprehension so strongly that in this Mississippi legislature, they voluntarily sat together on the opposite side of the Assembly to those crypto-Republicans. And they set up a passionate chorus of protest whenever one of the Greeley Republicans rose to speak.

Governor Ames had the instincts of a reformer. He cut the state debt drastically—a fact his enemies tried to conceal—and he accomplished this without sacrificing the provisions for the poor, the insane, the deaf, dumb, and blind. He was helped by the fact that the cotton crop reached its prewar standard in 1873.

No election in American history had such an immediate effect of thrusting the past into the future while leaving the present confused and frightened.

The election of 1876, which would shake the very foundations of social change, was still a full term away.

Six new Negro congressmen presented themselves in Washington. They came from South Carolina, Florida, Alabama, and Mississippi. Pinchback arrived from Louisiana as both senator-elect and representative-elect. His election to both offices had been verified. The quandary was temporarily met by questioning his credentials which were impeccable.

"Young, charming, daring," was what Washington said, as he settled down to wait. "He is about thrity-seven years old," said the *New York Commercial Advertiser,* "not darker than an Arab. . . . His features are regular, his eyes intensely black and brilliant. . . .Mr. Pinchback is the best dressed Southern man we have had in Congress since the days when gentlemen were Democrats."

Pinchback had to wait for three years. An extra session of Congress was almost entirely given to the thorny problem of Pinchback. The real problem, however (according to those who claimed to know), was the reluctance of senators' wives to entertain Mrs. Pinchback.

Sumner offered his Civil Rights Bill to a noisy, indifferent chamber. The former Vice-President of the Confederacy, Alexander Stephens, of Georgia, old and ailing, made a bitter attack against it in the House. The thin old tones had barely died away before Robert Elliott, congressman from South Carolina, seized the floor.

Elliott was as dark as Stephens was white. With his background of English schooling, Elliott was better educated. He was twenty-eight years old, a linguist, a lawyer, with one of the largest libraries in South Carolina.

He spoke with passion and cogency of the Negroes' share in American history. He held the floor until adjournment and this gave him the right to continue speaking the next day.

That night, everyone in Washington seemed to know that "the Anglo-Saxon and the African" had stood face to face.

When the session began the next day, the galleries of the House were filled with people who had stood in line since early morning. Senators stood around the walls to listen. Everyone waited impatiently for the sound of the arrival of Stephens' wheelchair and the beginning of the session.

Elliott did not disappoint them. He was eloquent, pungent, even humorous, and he spoke as a Negro and as an American. "I am what I am and I believe in my own nobility."

It was a personal triumph. It was to many an unforgettable moment in this chamber which had heard so many defenses of slavery. When Elliott sat down, the session did not resume until all his admirers—and some were reluctant Democrats—had shaken his hand.

For the next session of Congress, Elliott was Speaker of the House.

☆ 12 ☆

IN SEPTEMBER 1873, New York banks collapsed as though a pin had been thrust into a balloon. Jay Cooke, who had financed the Northern Pacific Railway and was inextricably tied to all railroad building, to unrestricted trade, inflated credit, unrestrained capital—failed, and the failure set off wave after wave of panic.

All the charges of fraud which had been used so freely during the campaign, became now the most living of truths. The effect of the panic and the business depression which followed brought an age to an end—an age of free and undisciplined enterprise, as high as the sky. Nearly one-fifth of the railway mileage now went into the hands of receivers. Industry stiffened and buttressed itself. The great corporations began their rule of undisputed power. Coal, steel, oil, copper became more important than any number of small, vulnerable men.

Raw materials in quantities never equaled before and markets unlimited assumed astronomical dimensions. Investment capital was available in the millions. Now investors must be guaranteed. Raw materials and markets unlimited could not be trusted to economic freebooters. They were stripped of their last rag of affectionate quasi-respectability.

The wan kind of democracy that went with freebootery was now associated exclusively with the Irish, the eastern Europeans arriving by the boatloads, the Negroes. Self-government was all very admirable but best understood and practiced by native born, white, Protestant Americans.

The panic and its remedies remade the Republican party. Old terms acquired new meanings. Liberalism was transformed into the fight against thievery in high places, and high thievery was represented as government in the hands of undisciplined men: men maintained in power by an evil affinity, North and South.

For nearly ten years, the principle of human equality though manifested in crude and fumbling ways, had been the motivating power. Those years were drawing to a close.

Some of the Radical Republicans who had believed that

a peaceful revolution was possible saw what was developing so ominously, but they were old men, few in number, and they were facing new men, ten feet tall.

When Congress met in December 1873, Sumner was no longer admitted as a Republican. Because of his repudiation of Grant and his last-minute endorsement of Greeley, the party managers decreed that he must sit among the Democrats.

It did not seem to matter to him very much. His Civil Rights Bill was perennially with him. In spite of his appearance as a great old animal near its end, he was kept alive by many fears.

Appointments to the Supreme Court in 1872 and 1873 had been cause for great concern. Corporation lawyers from Pennsylvania and New York had made the Court even more conservative than usual. In April 1873, the Slaughter House Cases showed that the Supreme Court intended to give the most limited interpretation possible to the Fourteenth Amendment. This case did not deal with Negroes at all. It was brought by certain butchers in New Orleans who maintained that a Louisiana statute giving exclusive slaughtering rights to certain parishes was unconstitutional. The plaintiffs claimed that the statute violated the Thirteenth and Fourteenth Amendments by creating a "servitude" upon those who were obliged to bring their animals to a designated slaughterhouse, thus abridging privileges and immunities of citizens of the United States. The Court answered by defining the rights of federal citizenship so narrowly that the protection of most civil rights was put back on the states which was exactly what the conservatives wanted.

Thus, within the five years of its life, the privileges and immunities clause of the Fourteenth Amendment was "divested of its constitutional vitality" and "privileges and immunities" were never applied to protect a civil right.

Sumner begged for his bill. "My desire, the darling desire of my soul at this moment is to close forever this great question so that it shall never again intrude into these chambers—so that hereafter in all our legislation there shall be no such words as 'black' or 'white' but that we shall speak only of citizens and of men."

He was refused.

By 1874, only four southern states were still governed by Radical Republicans: South Carolina, Florida, Louisiana and Mississippi.

In Louisiana, General McEnery, who had held the State House until put out by federal troops, said simply, "We shall carry the next election if we have to ride saddle-deep in blood to do it."

In May, forty men arranged for the next election. They were delegates from all the secret organizations. The place of meeting was alleged to be Magazine Street in New Orleans, although others insisted it was in the little town of Opelousas, Louisiana. By July, the Louisiana White League showed signs of being thoroughly reorganized under five new leaders. In August, several Negroes and Republican officeholders were killed at Coushatta, Louisiana. The governor declared martial law. By fall, the White League claimed 40,000 members.

All over the South this long hot summer, men saw warnings and intimations all about them. Sleep was broken by the pounding hoofs of horses in the night.

In South Carolina, the Negroes in the legislature were alarmed by the candid peculations of the aristocratic scalawag, Governor Moses. Since they were in the majority, this put them in a vulnerable position. The leading Negroes in the two houses appointed a joint commission to determine the exact situation. "Tax unions" were being formed by white conservatives to challenge and dispute all expenditures.

The commission brought financial sheets to prove that the cost of government had increased only thirty-eight cents per capita, that the state debt had been increased only five million dollars, and that this was due to the need to rebuild public utilities destroyed by the war, and to care for the new schools, asylums, prisons, and orphanages.

More and more South Carolina white men were leaving the Republicans and joining the Democrats and the "Tax unions." "Old men in the tax unions; young men in the rifle clubs," was the slogan heard all over the state.

The Negroes desperately needed the support of the whites who were now leaving them. Under the circumstances they had only two choices: build up and reform the party which had given them the vote or start a new organization. Men like Cardozo, the State Treasurer, and Robert Smalls provided the strongest Republican leadership. To them, charges of graft were not as important as strengthening the party which offered the only economic and civil protection. Their apprehensions were electrically alive. "Reform" had become a word like "liberal"—turned about, it destroyed Negro hopes.

In March 1874, Sumner died. His enemies were stronger than he could battle; his friends were few. Congressional friends had remained with him through the last day of his life. Negro friends, Frederick Douglass, George Downing, Sumner Wormley heard his hoarse whisper, spoken over and over, "You must take care of the Civil Rights Bill—my bill, the Civil Rights Bill—don't let it fail!"

"He was the conscience of the Senate," said Ralph Waldo Emerson.

Frederick Douglass led the three hundred Negroes who walked behind Sumner's body to the railway station. In Boston, colored soldiers stood on guard while the body lay in the State House.

The Senate passed his bill—perhaps out of courtesy to a dead colleague?—but it did not survive the House.

In June, the Freedmen's Bank came to an end, very quietly. It had fallen into the hands of sharpers and speculators. Jay Cooke & Company and the First National Bank of Washington apparently had the run of it. Nearly three million dollars were owed to Negro depositors. The intrinsic loss was small in comparison with the psychological shock to the Negroes who had been assured that they must demonstrate thrift through savings in order to prove that they were worthy of citizenship.

A sage and simple admonition was the text in the state campaigns that fall: "Let the good men of the South have a chance to work out their own destiny." In Alabama, a "campaign for liberation" took place. Its gunfire was directed against Negroes and registered Republicans.

A Democrat became governor: Democrats claimed the legislature, but the Republicans refused to agree in face of the statewide terror.

Thirty-five Negroes were elected from the Black Belt counties where the militia had protected the voters.

In Vicksburg, Mississippi, seven groups of the White League were formed to control the city election. The issue was twofold: "Too many niggers in office. Extravagance in building school houses."

Patrols took over the city. The sound of their feet kept voters awake in the night. Negroes stayed away from the polls; even so, nearly two hundred Negroes were killed in the counties surrounding Vicksburg.

In South Carolina, the new reform Republican governor, Chamberlain, attempted to clean house immediately and for a time it seemed as though he might be able to unite South Carolina, for the problems had nothing mysterious about them. The situation was summed up by an aristocratic legislator, Major F. F. Warley: "Save the state not from ignorant and corrupt legislators, so much as from rich, aspiring and unprincipled men, some of them imported it is true, but many of them degenerate and unworthy sons of that noble though now impoverished mother whom they rob."

In Florida, the governor elected by the planters died, and the lieutenant governor did his best to oust the Negro leader and Superintendent of Education, Jonathan C.

Gibbs. But Gibbs was too strong, although according to his brother, a judge in Arkansas, Gibbs slept in the attic of his home, which resembled an arsenal. "He said that for better advantage, it had been his resting place for several months as his life had been threatened by the Klan." Gibbs, in perfect health, suddenly died. His brother thought it was apoplexy, others thought he had been poisoned.

South Carolina, Louisiana, Mississippi had fought hard for the governors they now had—men with reputations for honesty and concern for civil rights. But these men faced legislatures dominated by extreme conservatives. In Louisiana, the State Democratic National Convention identified itself as "We, the white people of Louisiana." In Alabama, a Republican governor was elected but two legislatures claimed to have power. The Democrats gathered in the State House, the Republicans at the United States Court House. Through Grant's compromise plan, the Republicans gained a majority. In Texas, the State Supreme Court declared the election of a Democrat fraudulent. Negro militias refused to allow Democrats to take possession of the State House. Grant was asked for military aid which he refused, and the Republicans withdrew to prevent further bloodshed.

North Carolina was completely dominated by the Democrats. The Republicans made no appeal. The state had been lost to Reconstruction in 1870.

That November, in New York, Boss Tweed was convicted of stealing, with his partners, nearly $75,000,000 from the public.

But this was not the worst news of all. The worst news came as November moved into December and the counting at the polls was completed. Republican strongholds like Pennsylvania, Ohio, Massachusetts went to the Democrats. For the first time since 1861, the House was now controlled by the Democrats, and the Republican control of the Senate was too tenuous to be of much account.

As a footnote to history, Andrew Johnson returned to Congress as a senator from Tennessee. He made one fiery speech out of the past and died the next year.

Negroes met in convention in Montgomery, Alabama, in December, to consider their plight. "It is absolutely essential to our protection in our civil and political rights that the laws of the United States shall be enforced so as to compel respect and obedience for them. Before the state laws and state courts we are utterly helpless."

In Vicksburg, five hundred members of a "committee of taxpayers" took over the sheriff's office and the office of public records. Governor Ames called on the captain of the Negro militia to put out the invaders.

Both sides agreed to a parley, but as the Negroes withdrew, they were fired upon and thirty-five died.

Since "committees on taxation" were assuming the prerogatives of the "rifle clubs" in other parts of the state, Governor Ames wired President Grant for federal assistance.

Grant replied, "The public are tired out with these autumnal outbreaks in the South and the great majority are ready now to condemn any interference on the part of the government."

Grant was a tired and disillusioned man. In his message to Congress, he acknowledged that public opinion was strongly against the use of federal troops and yet without it, Negro suffrage would be worse than a mockery.

On December 21, he ordered troops into Mississippi.

One liability of a military man is the surprise to which he is subjected when authority does not bear its fruits; the law protected voters, the President enforced it—yet voters were still being whipped and killed. In February 1875, Grant asked Congress for a bill to protect voters in United States elections. He referred to the massacre at Colfax when he said, "Mississippi is today governed by officials chosen through fraud and violence such as would scarcely be credited to savages."

The bill was not passed. The Speaker of the House, James G. Blaine, was being mentioned for the Republican nomination. He told John Roy Lynch, the Negro congressman from Mississippi, that he was afraid such a bill would defeat the party throughout the country.

Conscience was lightened, however, by the passing of the Civil Rights Bill. In it, "all persons" within the United States "shall be entitled to the full and equal enjoyment of the accommodations, advantages, facilities and privileges of inns, public conveyances on land or water, theatres and other places of public amusement; subject only to the conditions and limitations established by law and applicable alike to citizens of every race and color regardless of any previous condition of servitude."

It was not exactly the bill Sumner had struggled to obtain. There were two interesting omissions: cemeteries and schools remained segregated.

From the moment it was passed, it was ignored. A Louisiana paper warned that "any Negro or gang of Negroes who attempted to act on the bill would do so at their peril."

In Alabama, when a Common Carrier Bill supplementing the larger bill in specifics was heading for defeat in the state legislature, Negroes and their white friends held rallies and boarded all the streetcars in Mobile from which they were normally excluded.

But the bill came too late. No pretense of enforcing the Civil Rights Bill in the South was ever made, and within eight years it was declared unconstitutional by the Supreme Court.

When the new session of Congress opened in March 1875, Blanche Kelso Bruce took his oath as senator from Mississippi.

Bruce had been born a slave in Virginia. He was now thirty-four years old, "with a magnificent physique," according to Washington comments, and a good education gotten at Oberlin College. He had gone to Mississippi in

1868, bought land, and begun to take part in state politics.

He was chairman of a number of congressional committees and he often presided over the Senate. He defended the Indians—who needed defending if any group did—and defended the Chinese who were not allowed American citizenship. He struggled valiantly for flood control of the Mississippi which regularly washed away life and property.

He was a literate, attractive man who found social life in Washington very difficult.

Grant was venturing some muffled hopes that peace had come. Goodness knows what he based them on, unless it was his own snatching at trifles. Any three consecutive weeks without a crisis was a miracle.

In South Carolina, Governor Chamberlain was impressing the state as "a model governor" *(Charlotte Observer)*, "fulfilling the pledges made alike to conservative and Republican" *(The Grange)*.

A public meeting in Charleston thanked him "for the bold and statesmanlike struggle" he had made "in the cause of reform and the economic administration of the government."

This was beyond dispute. He had already saved the state nearly two million dollars and had taken a firm hand against grafters. But "reform" still offered some semantic difficulties to men like Robert Elliott, who was growing deeply distrustful of the white Southerners who were offering Chamberlain their support: Elliott was greatly alarmed by the cuts in social spending. He was also alarmed because Chamberlain disbanded the Negro militia in a country where the militia was badly needed, had given tax relief to planters, had appointed several new judges from among conservative lawyers.

The Negroes of South Carolina had received a more extensive education in self-government than in perhaps any other reconstructed state. They even had one strong labor union, the Longshoremen's Protective Association of Charleston, which had carried on several strikes and won. A state labor convention had been held in Columbia, in 1869, with Robert Elliott as president. One-half share of crops for farm laborers was asked, or a wage of seventy cents to one dollar a day. They wanted a commissioner to protect labor contracts and prevent the legal delays in trying to recover wages or shares in crops. They wanted to secure laws protecting a laborer from being discharged without payment of wages and crops being sold before a satisfactory settlement had been made.

The cohesiveness and political acumen of the South Carolina Negroes made them, even on a bright day, prepare for a storm.

That summer, the Klan was comparatively quiet. Moderate men congratulated themselves, somewhat windily. Rumors that conservative Southerners had turned their faces against violence and planned other means of evading Negro suffrage were abstracted in such a way that the first clause was heard while the second trailed off.

The Republicans were expressing the belief that the time was near for the southern states to manage their own affairs. Grant was heard to murmur that force breeds force. As a soldier, he was eagerly awaiting the moment when provocative federal uniforms could be entirely withdrawn—at which signal the South would unreservedly turn to building its own industries.

From Yazoo City came a cry to Governor Ames. "I beg you send the United soldiers here, they have hung six more men; they wont let the republican have no ticket; fighting co comemense just I were closuing, 2 two killed . . . help, send troops and arms pleas . . . Send help help troops."

Three days later, in Clinton, Mississippi, fifteen hundred Negroes and one hundred whites were holding a Republican barbecue. Five hundred armed white men, arriving in a special train, stampeded the crowd, destroyed food and wagons, stole mules and horses, fired into the crowd, and killed from fifty to eighty people.

Governor Ames wired for help. Grant refused.

Now events moved with a terrible speed. "The time has come," the *Clarion* said, "when companies that have been organized for protective and defensive purposes should come to the front. . . . Let every citizen hold himself in readiness to join one of these companies."

"The shameless, heartless, vile, grasping, deceitful, creeping, crawling, wallowing, slimy, slippery, hideous, loathsome political pirates must be wiped out."

Mississippi became such a nightmare in that lovely fall of 1875 that the governor saw nothing ahead but a holocaust. A "peace agreement" was presented by the Democrats and he signed it.

The arms and ammunition were not distributed. The Negro militias were disbanded.

The Democrats had promised to protect the Negro voters.

They did indeed. They made sure they stayed at home. Yazoo City, in 1873, had two thousand four hundred and twenty-seven Republican votes, in 1875, seven. In a few towns, however, Negroes were reported to have marched to the polling places "after the manner of soldiers armed with clubs and sticks; some of them with old swords and pieces of scythe blades."

The legislature was lost to the Democrats. County officials were metamorphosed into Democrats.

Governor Ames and Lieutenant Governor A. K. Davis, a Negro, were forced to escape from the state to save their lives.

Congress sent a committee to investigate.

It concluded that the current legislature was not a legal body, that the state had fallen "under the control of political organizations composed largely of armed men whose common purpose is to deprive the Negro of the free exercise of the right of suffrage and to establish and maintain the supremacy of the white-line Democracy."

It was called the "Mississippi Plan for the Restoration of Home Rule."

One state legislator was shot down on the streets of Clinton. Another was hanged by the White League. A third was shot in broad daylight. A fourth was killed in the court house at Yazoo City. The body of a fifth was pulled out of a water hole. All were men who had been active in the state since the constitutional convention. Houses of Negro Republicans were broken into, and if the inhabitants escaped alive to the woods they were fortunate.

In Louisiana, a "butchery of citizens" took place "which in barbarity is hardly surpassed by an act of savage warfare."

Everywhere the Negro was left standing alone while his white allies took refuge in the Democratic ranks. In the North, there were ashen faces, grim lips, and eyes averted.

It was desperately unfortunate, terribly inexplicable, frightfully embarrassing. But what could be done? Spend another decade trying to hound people into democracy? Federal troops had never yet won a Presidential election, and nominating conventions were meeting in less than four months.

The new governor of Mississippi, installed by "home rule," soon defaulted to the sound of $316,000.

The Republicans nominated Rutherford B. Hayes of Ohio, as a compromise candidate to quiet the scandals. He had once said of government, "It is not the government of any class or sect or nationality or race . . . it is not the government of the native born or of the foreign born, of the rich man or the poor man, of the white man or of the colored man—it is the government of the free man."

The Democrats nominated Samuel J. Tilden, a reform governor of New York, who had broken the Tweed ring. He was confident he would win.

In August 1876, the Mississippi Plan formally moved

into South Carolina. Wade Hampton, who had been living on his Mississippi plantation, returned to his native state at the earnest solicitation of his friends. Wade Hampton, who had been a Confederate general, was a gentleman, a responsible man; he would control the hoodlums who carried the burning crosses. This was a cogent and popular argument with other responsible men.

Hampton laid out the campaign. He wrote, "Every Democrat must feel honor bound to control the vote of at least one Negro, by intimidation, purchase, keeping away, or as each individual may determine how he may best accomplish it. . . . Never threaten a man individually. If he deserves to be threatened, the necessities of the times require that he should die."

At Hamburg, South Carolina, a practical application of this philosophy took place in July. Grant, asking once more for congressional intervention, described it as: "A disgraceful and brutal slaughter of unoffending men . . . a scene as cruel, bloodthirsty, wanton, unprovoked, and as uncalled for as it was, is only a repetition of the course that has been pursued in other states within the last few years, notably in Mississippi and Louisiana. . . . Murders and massacres of innocent men for opinion's sake, or on account of color, have been of too frequent occurrence to require recapitulation of testimony here. All are familiar with their horrible details, the only wonder being that so many justify them or apologize for them."

It was an agonizing experience for this man. He himself was discredited by the excesses of his administration. The Republicans were afraid to raise the issue of Negro rights with the voters. It was worn out as an election device. Extreme apathy—even lack of sympathy—was recognized by those sensitive barometers, campaign managers. And Supreme Court decisions merely confirmed them.

Appeal cases reached the Supreme Court as a part of election tactics. In United States vs. Reese, it was held that state legislation in Kentucky which penalized anyone obstructing a citizen from voting was unconstitutional. Once more the Fifteenth Amendment was held to the narrowest interpretation. In the United States vs. Cruikshank, the Court set aside the convictions of men indicted for breaking up a gathering of Negroes in which several Negroes were killed. Although it did not declare the specific civil rights statute unconstitutional, it narrowed federal protection almost to a vanishing point.

The Civil War was being fought all over again, but it had suffered an extraordinary sea-change. The Reconstruction measures were damned with violent epithets. Federal "interference" in the form of the Civil Rights Bill, the right of states to determine the qualified voters were discussed up hill and down by the Democrats and sidestepped by the Republicans. It was a miserable campaign in which Hayes and Tilden flung libelous charges at each other, and Tilden called for the repeal of the Fifteenth Amendment.

The killings were hushed up or not mentioned or justified or made the inevitable reaction of civilized men facing African savagery.

"Does any sane man believe the Negro capable of comprehending the Ten Commandments? The miraculous conception and birth of our Saviour? . . ." one Democratic legislator asked.

"Every effort to inculcate these great truths but tends to brutalize his nature, and by obfuscating his little brain unfits him for the duties assigned him as hewer of wood and drawer of water. The effort makes him a demon of wild fanatical destruction, and consigns him to the fatal shots of the white man."

It was a public secret that the election would probably be very close. If the southern states could be carried by Tilden, he would be the next President. The House made a formal request to Grant that he enforce the law protecting voters. He promptly sent troops into South Caroilna, ordered the disbanding of "rifle clubs," ordered Sheridan, commanding the Texas-Louisiana sector, to keep peace at all costs. Grant, himself, kept up a steady appeal to Southerners to take the initiative, stop the terror, make federal interference unnecessary.

Poor Grant. Everything he did seemed merely to expose his own tragic position. A man who had won two landslide victories was abandoned and vilified. Few other Presidents have ever had such an experience. He was threatened with impeachment; scandals surrounded his official family and his unofficial friends. He was the center of such a complex of venality and false virtue, that it is amazing he kept any shred of his dignity. The anti-Grant majority in Congress appointed committee after committee to investigate the administration, and virtue became such a dazzling Democratic ornament that the poor Republicans were blinded.

Tilden needed South Carolina and Louisiana baldy. John Sherman, member of Congress from Ohio for many years, wrote that anarchy rode the election. "Organized clubs of masked armed men, formed as recommended by the central Democratic committee, rode through the country at night, marking their course by the whipping, shooting, wounding, maiming, mutilation and murder of women, children, and defenseless men whose houses were forcibly entered. . . . Crimes like these, testified to by scores of witnesses, were the means employed in Louisiana to elect a President of the United States."

In South Carolina, Federal troops intervened in a riot in Aiken County. "No one ever knew how many were killed," said the report, but the estimate was between eighty and one hundred and twenty-five. In Charleston County, in October, Negroes killed five white men and wounded sixteen others.

In Edgefield County, South Carolina, armed men packed the steps and corridors of the court house to prevent a Negro leader and several hundred Republicans with him from voting. The federal officer requested General Gary, Hampton's campaign manager, to hear the Negroes'

171

vigorous protest. Gray's reply was reported to be, "By God, sir, I'll not do it. I will keep the compact I made with you this morning that white men and Negroes should vote at separate boxes."

What this meant, in fact, had been demonstrated in Mississippi and Louisiana. There, "separate boxes" meant that, as Lerone Bennett, Jr., writes, "polling places were located in bayous and on islands, in barns and fodder houses. Armed white men were stationed on the roads leading to the polls. In one Louisiana parish, the polling place was located in an isolated wilderness. The whites gathered at the white church and were told, in whispers, how to reach the polls. In another county, the polls opened in the dark of morning and whites voted by light of candles. When the Negro voters showed up, the polls were closed for the day. In Mississippi, white men from Alabama and Louisiana streamed across the state lines and voted early and often."

Charles Foster, congressman from Ohio and a powerful supporter of Hayes, said in a Louisiana speech that if Mr. Hayes were elected, he would "wipe out sectional lines; under him, the flag would wave over states, not provinces; over free men, not subjects."

It was an effective bid. It cut down any difference between Hayes and Tilden. On November 7, Hayes went to bed at midnight convinced he had lost the election. Next morning, the *New York Times* agreed that Tilden had won. But Hayes, fixing his cool wide-awake morning eyes on four doubtful states—South Carolina, Louisiana, Florida, and Oregon—had second thoughts about victory.

If only one of these states was credited to Tilden, Tilden would indeed win, but both Republicans and Democrats claimed to have won the election in Louisiana, Florida, and South Carolina.

Once more, dual governments were set up.

On November 9, federal troops moved into Florida. The Republicans sent up a great shout that Tilden would never occupy the White House. The Democrats laughed at them. If the count were thrown into the House of Representatives, with its large Democratic majority, Tilden would undoubtedly receive the election.

There was talk that the country was on the verge of civil war. Rumors were cheaper than beer. Rumors said that Democrats would march on Washington and seize the government.

Grant concentrated troops in and around the city. Arsenals were guarded. Known trouble-makers were watched. Every precaution was taken to prevent action from fire-eaters of either side.

As the days went on through November into December, the tension mounted all through the country. It was known that intense negotiations of some kind were going on. Louisiana Democrats arranged a filibuster of one hundred and sixteen congressmen to prevent a count of the electoral vote. This threat of filibuster hung so menacingly over Congress that strenuous efforts were made to break the impasse.

There was anguished uncertainty as to who would count the electoral vote and whether the electoral counters should go "behind the state returns" to establish their validity. At last an electoral commission of ten congressmen was agreed on. Five associate justices of the Supreme Court were selected to break any deadlock.

The vote was a solemn performance reaching over the weeks. It came to its climax at four in the morning of March 2—two days before a President was to be inaugurated.

The electoral vote went to Hayes.

A majority of Americans considered it a "stolen election." Not until long afterward were the details known.

The South had suffered more from the 1873 panic than any other section of the country. The South desperately needed federal subsidies. Hayes desperately needed electoral votes. The southern Democrats, unknown to their northern colleagues, agreed to support Hayes if the subsidies were promised.

But while matters were still in the stage of private negotiation, the powerful *Ohio State Journal* printed a bitter editorial against the South. It shook the negotiations so seriously that Hayes had to make further concessions.

Four days later, on February 26, 1876, three private conferences took place. Two were in Capitol committee rooms, the final and conclusive one, in a hotel.

The final agreement was simply that if Rutherford B. Hayes were confirmed as President, he would permit the Democrats to control the state governments of Louisiana, Florida, and Mississippi. The remaining troops would be immediately withdrawn, and the states returned to the jurisdiction of white legislators.

The next day, the agreement was confirmed by F. H. Nicholls of Louisiana, the Democrat who claimed the governor's chair. He was assured that Grant had already been notified of the need to modify his enforcement order. Nicholls, guarded by the White League, took his oath of office.

Hayes took a private oath the next day, Saturday, March 3. His public inauguration would take place on Monday. It was agreed that Grant should not leave the White House untenanted over the weekend, and there was profound relief when the transfer was completed on the fifth.

On April 10, federal troops were withdrawn from Columbia, South Carolina, and Wade Hampton became governor. Ten days later, all troops were withdrawn from New Orleans. In January, the Republicans were driven from the Florida legislature by order of the State Supreme Court.

It would have been much harder for Tilden, the Democrat, to accomplish these ends. For Hayes, a Republican, it was merely a matter of using the telegraph.

Hayes was defensive when a friend reproached him. He had no choice. Public opinion was against any further intervention in the South. At the Washington conference, he had in fact given up something which Republicans no longer possessed.

Public reaction comforted itself that Nicholls had solemnly agreed to allow the Louisiana Negro to keep his vote and not to deprive the Negro child of an education.

It took a few years to accomplish both deprivations, for the desire for independence lay deep.

☆ 13 ☆

IN THE CONGRESS elected that year, only four Republicans came from the South. The ninety-seven other southern congressmen were Democrats.

Northern Republicans like Blaine protested that something was wrong. They knew very well what it was, but they had surrendered their power to change it.

The Democrats launched a whole series of "riders" to administration bills designed to starve the administration into a complete withdrawal of marshals and deputy marshals from southern elections now or in the future.

Hayes vetoed the measures, but such confusion followed that the government ground to a virtual halt until special sessions were called to start the machinery going again.

Wade Hampton in South Carolina, like F. T. Nicholls

in Louisiana, had promised to protect the Negro voters. Seventeen Negro Republican representatives, duly elected, were immediately expelled from the South Carolina legislature, and Democrats replaced them in a special election.

In ten years, Negroes had learned to be voters. It would take another generation to unteach them through social and economic starvation.

D. L. Chamberlain, who had been South Carolina's reform Republican governor, wrote in the *Atlantic Monthly* some years later, "Every present citizen of South Carolina knows, and those who are truthful and frank will confess, that the ballot debauched in 1876, remains debauched: the violence taught then, remains now, if not in the same, then in other forms. The defiance of law learned then in what was called a good cause survives in the horrid orgies of degradations and of lynchings."

The price paid was the defacement of the United States. The price was a loss of spiritual values which made us vulnerable in ways we could not afford.

The planters had not been afraid of bad Negro legislators. They had been afraid of good ones. Genuine equality was the crime of those days.

An editorial in *The Floridian,* in 1873, said, "No greater calamity could befall the state of Florida while under the rule of its present officials than to be placed in good financial credit . . . Our only hope is the state's utter financial bankruptcy, and heaven grant that may speedily come."

Negro militia and police were forcibly disarmed.

Public education was almost destroyed by appropriation of school funds. In 1879, Virginia used $1,000,000 allocated to the schools for other purposes. The Georgia legislature made invalid $350,000 worth of bonds belonging to the school funds.

Fragments of political power remained to the Negro for another twenty years. But jobs did not come with the assertion of political rights. Family security depended on being a "safe nigger."

"Grandfather" clauses and white primaries made the effort to vote hardly worth the penalties that would follow.

The massive philosophy of racial inferiority which had been raised to such a polished state in slavery days was reaffirmed: the Negro had had his chance and showed how venal and irresponsible he was ...

Most effective of all was the suppression of records and the rewriting of history. Records vanished in Florida, South Carolina, Louisiana, and Mississippi. Historians in the next generation mutilated facts with almost unparalleled concentration and adroitness.

Poor and ineffective Negroes were essential to the social myth and imperative to maintain wage differentials. Yet low wages for Negroes meant low wages for white men. A state poor in its spending power was a state poor in all the benefits it had to offer.

It is impossible to segregate poor health and debased living: both are highly infectious. A concentrated philosophy of debasement acquires a peculiar life of its own; it abandons reality. It stands on one foot and imagines it is walking.

Schools were maintained in some fashion, mostly through the devotion of teachers who refused to be intimidated.

The reconstructed governments had lasted for scarcely a wink of an eye: the longest, in South Carolina, lived for seven years, in Mississippi, for six, in Georgia and North Carolina the governments survived for two years.

Of the Negro men who had made the governments:

Dr. Martin Delaney, of South Carolina, went to South America to act as agent for a Boston mercantile firm.

Robert Elliott was appointed by the former senator from Ohio, John Sherman, who had become Hayes' Secretary of the Treasury, to be a special agent of the Treasury in Charleston. His enemies were determined to get him out, and they succeeded. He died when he was forty-two.

Francis Cardozo was also given an appointment by Secretary of the Treasury Sherman in Washington, and served for six years. Then he became principal of the colored high school of Washington which had 250 students—"200 female and 50 male."

The Reverend Richard Cain remained in Congress until 1883. After that, the Methodist Church elected him a bishop assigned to the Louisiana-Texas district. He became president of Quinn College in Waco, Texas.

Beverly Nash was an elector during the Hayes campaign. He was said to have been offered $100,000 to vote for Tilden, which he refused. After that, he goes into obscurity.

Jeremiah Haralson, in Alabama, tried vainly to run for state office in 1878 and 1884. He held unimportant federal offices at irregular intervals. In time he left the South and went to Colorado. There he was killed by wild animals in 1916.

Blanche K. Bruce was made registrar of the United States Treasury by President James Garfield and, through his executive ability, held the post for many years.

Hiram Revels became president of Alcorn University in Rodney, Mississippi.

Thomas E. Miller, a Negro who had sat with the South Carolina lawmakers, made an eloquent speech at the convention which, in 1895, disfranchised him formally.

". . . starting as infants in legislation in 1869, many wise measures were not thought of, many injudicious acts were passed. But in the administration of affairs for the next four years, having learned by experience the result of bad acts, we immediately passed reformatory laws touching every department of state, county, municipal and town government. These enactments are today upon the statute books. They stand as living witness of the Negro's fitness to vote and legislate upon the rights of mankind . . .

"We were eight years in power. We built schoolhouses, established charitable institutions, built and maintained the penitentiary system, provided for the education of the deaf and dumb, rebuilt the jails and courthouses, rebuilt the bridges and reestablished the ferries. In short, we reconstructed the state and placed it upon the road to prosperity and, at the same time, by our acts of financial reform, transmitted to the Hampton government an indebtedness not greater by more than $2,500,000 than was the bonded debt of the state in 1860, before the Republican Negroes and their white allies came to power."

When John Roy Lynch, who had served in Congress from Mississippi, was counted out of his election, he said, "The impartial historian will record the fact that the colored people of the South have contended for their rights with a bravery and a gallantry that is worthy of the highest commendation. Being, unfortunately, in dependent circumstances with the preponderance of the wealth against them, they have refused to surrender their honest convictions even upon the altar of their present necessities."

The constitutions adopted by the "black and tan" legislatures remained on the statute books in most states. In Florida, no change was made for seventeen years, in Virginia, for thirty-two years, in South Carolina, for twenty-seven years, in Mississippi, for twenty-two years.

But in time, white teachers could not teach Negro students.

Mill workers in South Carolina were forbidden to look out the same window as whites.

Separate Bibles were offered Negro witnesses.

For seven years a majority of Americans acted on the conviction that men were equal. For the seven years of American history that is called Reconstruction, social and economic revolution was attempted on a scale never before envisioned by man. It was the struggle of fourteen million human beings to come up out of darkness into light.

Each law that spoke for education and equality, compassion and concern, each affirmation of dignity for all were mighty candles in that darkness. Though the candles had been put out, the darkness was no longer impenetrable for the light was carried in the mind.

The end was sure.

CHRONOLOGY

1865

January	Congress passes Thirteenth Amendment which, when ratified, abolished slavery.
February	First Negro admitted to practice before the United States Supreme Court. His name: John S. Rock, of Boston.
March	Freedmen's Bureau authorized by Congress.
April	Lincoln assassinated. Andrew Johnson becomes President.
May	Johnson offers amnesty to Confederates.
September	Thaddeus Stevens urges in Congress that estates of Confederate leaders be confiscated and distributed in forty-acre lots to freedmen.
Fall	In southern states, white legislators pass Black Codes, virtually re-enslaving the Negroes.
December	Congress constitutes Joint Committee on Reconstruction.

1866

February	Stevens tries again to get land for the freedmen, without success.
April	Johnson declares Civil War at an end except in Texas. Civil Rights Bill passed over Johnson's veto.
May	Riots, for three days, in Memphis, Tenn., destroying Negro lives and property.
July	Riot in New Orleans with heavy loss of life.
August	Johnson declares Civil War at an end in every part of the country including Texas.

January	Negroes allowed to vote in the District of Columbia—over Johnson's veto.
March	First Congressional Reconstruction Acts, designed to protect Negroes politically and economically. Constitutional conventions ordered, with Negroes participating fully in the elections.
April	Ku Klux Klan is formed in Nashville.

January	Constitutional conventions begin to meet in southern states, with Negroes fully participating.
June	Oscar J. Dunn, an ex-slave, becomes Lieutenant-Governor of Louisiana.
July	Fourteenth Amendment bestowing privileges and immunities of citizenship on everyone who, by birth or naturalization, is subject to the jurisdiction of the United States and the state in which he resides, is added to the Constitution.
August	Death of Thaddeus Stevens.

February	Hiram R. Revels of Mississippi becomes first Negro Senator, taking Jefferson Davis' seat.
March	Fifteenth Amendment, giving equal voters' rights to all citizens regardless of race, color, or previous condition of servitude, added to the Constitution.
May	Congress passes first series of Enforcement Acts designed to control the Klan and guarantee civil and political rights to Negroes through the Federal courts.
December	Joseph H. Rainey of South Carolina becomes the first Negro in the House of Representatives.

1871

October   President Grant suspends writ of habeas corpus in nine counties in South Carolina in an effort to stem the Klan.

1872

December   P. B. S. Pinchback becomes first Negro governor of a state (Louisiana) when governor is impeached.

1874

March   Death of Charles Sumner.
Summer   Terror throughout the South.
December   Grant issues proclamation on violence in Mississippi.

1875

March   Civil Rights Bill enacted by Congress. Blanche Kelso Bruce becomes second Negro Senator.
September   Mississippi governor asks for Federal troops to protect rights of Negro voters. Request refused.

1876

October   Grant orders Federal troops into South Carolina.

1877

February   Rutherford B. Hayes makes secret agreement to withdraw troops from the South in exchange for Southern electoral votes.
April   Troops withdrawn from South Carolina. Government returned to Democrats. Troops withdrawn from Louisiana and Florida.

BIBLIOGRAPHY

Allen, James S.: *Reconstruction: A Study in Democracy*. New York: International Publishers, 1937.

Aptheker, Herbert: *The Negro in the Civil War*. New York: International Publishers, 1938.

Bennett, Lerone, Jr.: *Before the Mayflower*. Chicago: Johnson Publishing Co., 1962.

Brodie, Fawn N.: *Thaddeus Stevens, Scourge to the South*. New York: W. W. Norton Company, Inc., 1959.

Donald, David H.: *The Scalawag in Mississippi*. Journal of Southern History, vol. 10.

DuBois, W. E. B.: *Black Reconstruction*. New York: Harcourt Brace & Co., 1935.

Eaton, John: *Grant, Lincoln and the Freedmen*. New York: Longmans, Green & Company, Inc., 1907.

Franklin, John Hope: *Reconstruction After the Civil War*. Chicago: University of Chicago Press, 1961.

Murray, Pauli: *Proud Shoes*. New York: Harper & Bros., 1956.

Olmsted, Frederick Law: *The Cotton Kingdom*. New York: Alfred A. Knopf, Inc., 1953.

Pierce, E. L.: *Memoirs and Letters of Charles Sumner*. Boston: Roberts Bros., 1893.

Roussève, Charles B.: *The Negro in Louisiana*. New Orleans: Xavier University Press, 1937.

Sandburg, Carl: *Abraham Lincoln: The War Years*. New York: Harcourt Brace & Co., 1939.

Scroggs, Jack B.: *Southern Reconstruction: A Radical View*. Lexington, Ky.: Journal of Southern History, vol. 24.

Schurz, Carl: *Reminiscences*. New York: McClure & Co., 1907–1908.

Sherman, John: *Recollections of Forty Years in the House*. Chicago: The Werner Co., 1895.

Skaggs, W. H.: *Southern Oligarchy*. New York: The Devin-Adair Co., 1924.

Simkins and Woody: *South Carolina Under Reconstruction*. Chapel Hill, University of North Carolina Press, 1932.

Wharton, Vernon Lane: *The Negro in Mississippi. 1865–1890*. Chapel Hill: University of North Carolina Press, 1947.

Wiley, B. I.: *Southern Negroes: 1861–1865*. New Haven: Yale University Press, 1938.

Woodson, Carter G.: *A Century of Negro Migration*. Washington: Association for the Study of Negro Life and History, 1918.

Woodward, C. Vann: *Reunion and Reaction*. New York: Anchor Books, Doubleday & Company, Inc., 1956.